MW00816535

"Naim Ateek's memoir, spanning the history of the Palestinian catastrophe and the birth of the state of Israel, is expansive in its breadth yet detailed in its markings. Through trial and tribulation, Ateek is firm and open, justice-seeking, and compassionate. We the readers embark with Ateek on a journey of despair and hope where faith is tried and honed."

—**MARC H. ELLIS**, author of *First Light: Encountering Edward Said and the Late-Style Jewish Prophetic in the New Diaspora*

CALL AND COMMITMENT

Call and Commitment

A Journey of Faith from Nakba to
Palestinian Liberation Theology

Naim Stifan Ateek

Foreword by Brian J. Grieves

CASCADE *Books* · Eugene, Oregon

CALL AND COMMITMENT
A Journey of Faith from Nakba to Palestinian Liberation Theology

Cascade Books
An Imprint of Wipf and Stock Publishers
199 W. 8th Ave., Suite 3
Eugene, OR 97401

www.wipfandstock.com

PAPERBACK ISBN: 978-1-6667-9897-5
HARDCOVER ISBN: 978-1-6667-9896-8
EBOOK ISBN: 978-1-6667-9898-2

Cataloguing-in-Publication data:

Names: Ateek, Naim Stifan, 1937–, author. | Grieves, Brian J., foreword.

Title: Call and commitment : a journey of faith from nakba to Palestinian liberation theology / Naim Stifan Ateek ; foreword by Brian J. Grieves.

Description: Eugene, OR : Cascade Books, 2023 | Includes bibliographical references and index.

Identifiers: ISBN 978-1-6667-9897-5 (paperback) | ISBN 978-1-6667-9896-8 (hardcover) | ISBN 978-1-6667-9898-2 (ebook)

Subjects: LCSH: Ateek, Naim Stifan, 1937–. | Liberation theology. | Christianity—Palestine. | Israel (Christian theology). | Palestine—Church history—20th century. | Palestine—Politics and government—1948–.

Classification: BT93.8 .A86 2023 (print) | BT93.8 .A86 (ebook)

11/01/23

To
Maha
Stefan, Christina, Lisa, Markus,
Sari, Tanory, Naeem, Mariam,
Nevart, Richard, Tristan

Contents

Part III: The Intifada and the Birth of Palestinian Liberation Theology

Part IV: Sabeel

Contents

Contents

Foreword

If a picture is worth a thousand words, the maps below are worth ten thousand words.

The British government first approved of the idea of a Jewish homeland in Palestine in 1917 in a document called the Balfour Declaration. Britain then assumed control of Palestine under the League of Nations' Mandate for Palestine.

The horrors of the Holocaust in the 1930s and '40s led many Western countries, out of feelings of guilt and a desire to atone, to justify the Zionist takeover of a part of historic Palestine. Zionists insisted that Palestine was a "land without a people, for a people without a land." But this was false. The Arabs of Palestine had lived on the land for centuries and were the indigenous people of the land.

According to an Ottoman census in 1878, the pre-Zionist population of Palestine was 472,455, with Muslims comprising 85.5 percent, Christians 9.2 percent, historic Jews 3.2 percent, and foreign-born Jews 2.1 percent. According to a British census in 1922 Palestine had a population of 752,000, of which 78 percent were Muslim, 11 percent Jewish, and 9 percent Christian.[1]

By 1948, the population of Palestine had risen to 1,900,000, with Jews, mostly Zionists, comprising about 32 percent of the population and Arabs 68 percent, and Jews had settled about 6 percent of the land[2] (see Map 1).

Then came the UN partition plan, which divided the land of historic Palestine, with 57 percent of the land for a Jewish state and the remaining 43 percent for an Arab state (see Map 2). The name "Israel" for the Jewish

1. "Demographic History of Palestine."
2. "Demographic History of Palestine"; "United Nations Special Committee."

state was not yet suggested by the provisional government of David Ben Gurion. This came later, between the time of the partition and establishment of the state.

Faced with losing more than half their land, the Partition Plan was rejected by Palestinians and the Arab league, who argued that the division of territory violated the UN principles of national self-determination.[3] War broke out in 1947 and the Zionists, armed from abroad, eventually claimed 78 percent of the land and the Palestinians were left with 22 percent. See Map 3, which shows the West Bank, including East Jerusalem, under Palestinian control, but ruled by Jordan, and the Gaza Strip ruled by Egypt. The Palestinians continued to dispute this dispossession of their land.

In June 1967, the six-day war erupted, and Israel occupied the remaining Palestinian areas. This occupation continues today, and Israeli expansion of Jewish settlements in the occupied areas has further dispossessed the Palestinians of all but a few cantons (see Map 4). In 1988 the Palestine Liberation Organization, relying on the Partition Plan UN resolution 181, declared Palestinian Independence on 22 percent of historic Palestine, within the borders of June 4, 1967. This they did in accordance with UN resolution 242. The International Court of Justice upheld the right of self-determination.[4]

This memoir by the Reverend Canon Naim Ateek, a Palestinian and an Episcopal priest, writes of the Palestinians dispossession of their land during that time as delineated in the maps below, leading Canon Ateek to embrace a groundbreaking theology of liberation for his people. Told in his own words, Canon Ateek weaves his personal story within the context of ever-increasing injustices endured by the Palestinian people during his lifetime. His story is a gift to all those who wish to understand what justice requires in the seventy-five years since the catastrophe that befell the Palestinian people in 1948.

The Reverend Canon Brian J. Grieves
Episcopal Church Peace and Justice Officer—Retired (1988–2009)

---

3. "United Nations Partition Plan."
4. "United Nations Partition Plan."

Disappearing Palestine

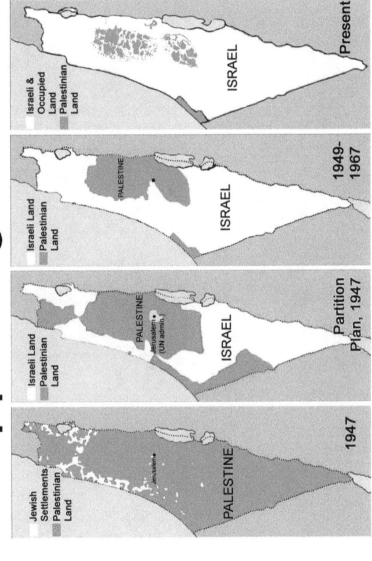

Jewish Settlements
Palestinian Land

1947

Israeli Land
Palestinian Land

PALESTINE
Jerusalem (UN admin.)
ISRAEL

Partition Plan, 1947

Israeli Land
Palestinian Land

PALESTINE
ISRAEL

1949–1967

Israeli & Occupied Land
Palestinian Land

ISRAEL

Present

Preface

My Sabeel[1] to Ministry

The gifts he gave were that some would be apostles, some prophets, some evangelists, some pastors and teachers, to equip the saints for the work of ministry, for building up the body of Christ. . . .

—EPHESIANS 4:11–12

WHEN I WAS BORN in 1937 the storms of a major world war were brewing. Nazism was on the rise and Zionism was on the move. Jewish-led militant groups were already planning the takeover of Palestine. These two cataclysmic events were certainly related, and the horrors of the Holocaust hastened the Zionist project. As a mere infant at the time, I was unaware of the impact these events would have on my life, and the lives of all Palestinians. I write this memoir to provide context for the eventual development of a Christian theology of liberation, which was my response to the injustice that befell the Palestinian people. This culminated in my book *Justice and Only Justice* in 1989. I will share more about that later in this telling. But suffice it to say that every experience in my life contributed to my eventual undertaking to provide a theology of liberation for my people.

For the first twenty-two years of my life, God was preparing me for my future ministry. I did not have the faintest idea how God's purpose would work out in my life, but I felt sure that God had called me, and that I must remain faithful to the call. Indeed, I had to keep walking my journey in the footsteps of Christ, in love, in faith, in trust, and in nonviolence.

1. Sabeel is an Arabic word that means "the way" or a spring of fresh water.

Whatever I have been able to accomplish has been done, undoubtedly, through Christ and for the glory of God. I have never dreamed of fame or prominence, but my dream and hope have always been clear from childhood: I wanted to be a servant of Jesus Christ.

When I was a student at Hardin-Simmons University in Abilene, Texas, I majored in chemistry, and I did well. One day my chemistry professor asked me what vocation I would be seeking when I left college. I immediately answered that I wanted to go into the ministry and become *Assis*[2] in the Episcopal Church in Palestine/Israel. She took an interest in me and occasionally we would discuss life in Nazareth and the Holy Land. She encouraged me to go to medical school. "You will make a fine doctor," she would say. She kept bringing it up and I would reply that I had always felt God's call for ministry. It became an embarrassment to keep saying "no" to her. Sometime later I told her that I would go to medical school and then go to seminary to study for the ministry. The sense of a call was very deep and real for me. It never wavered.

My mother used to tell me that ever since I was a little boy I would put on a shawl or stole around my shoulders and pretend I was Assis. The image of a person leading prayer and preaching the word of God must have been imprinted in my memory at a very early age. And yet to become an Assis of a church, as I discovered many years later, was only the first stage of the journey. What has been crucial has been walking in fidelity and trusting every step of the way. Long before I was humanly conscious of it, I used to say to my family that I wanted to be an Assis. I am sure God's call comes to people at various times and in various circumstances. For me, it came before I was personally conscious of it. I trust that in the foreknowledge of God, God knew it all. But I did not know it.

---

2. Assis or Qassis (in classical Arabic), is an Arabic word that means shepherd. It is the owner of the sheep and not the hireling that always looks after and cares for the sheep. In Aramaic/Syriac, Assis or Qassis means an "elder." In common usage, Assis is the pastor/minister/priest of the congregation.

Acknowledgments

HAVING OFFICIALLY RETIRED FROM Sabeel, Jerusalem, Maha and I decided to move to the States to be close to our grandchildren. A number of friends and family have occasionally encouraged me to write my memoir. When the right time came, and as best as I know how, I started to pen my story. A few months before the pandemic, with basic help from Cedar Duaybis and Tina Whitehead, I completed the draft of over three hundred pages and sent it to a few friends to read. I am thankful to Susan Bell, Leila Richards, and my son Sari, who took the time to read it. Although their feedback was encouraging, I felt that something was missing. I shared this with my friend Brian Grieves, who showed interest in looking it over, and suggested I send the manuscript to Sheryl Kujawa-Holbrook, dean of the Claremont School of Theology in California. It's important to note that Brian had previous experience in writing and editing books. When, later, Brian offered his help, I felt much more relaxed. About the same time, Wipf and Stock had accepted to publish my memoir. For the following two years, Brian helped rearrange the material, focusing mainly on the topic that I have chosen for my memoir. With the basic help of Brian and Tina, and occasional consultation with Cedar, and support of my daughter Nevart, we were able to finalize the manuscript. I am forever grateful to Brian for his expertise and Tina for her editing and computer skills. As always, I am thankful for Maha's constant encouragement; and above all for the grace and mercy of God.

Note: I have also decided to print a special booklet that can accompany the memoir for those who wish to have it. In addition to other miscellaneous material about Sabeel and Palestinian Liberation Theology, the booklet will contain some personal and family material that was not included in the memoir, as well as names of friends who have been part of my life's journey who I would like to recognize.

Part I

Early Years

1

The Nakba (the Catastrophe)[1]

OUR BEAUTIFUL LIFE IN Beisan was disrupted when the Jewish militias occupied Beisan on Wednesday, May 12, 1948. During the previous night there had been some exchange of fire between Arab Palestinians and Jewish Zionist soldiers, but there was no organized plan by the Arab Palestinians for defending the town. There was no army, no militia. After hearing about the massacre of Deir Yassin (April 9, 1948), some of the inhabitants of Beisan had decided to leave days before the town was occupied. Several families came to Father and Mother and left the keys of their homes with us and asked us to look after their homes until their return. Many people did not realize the seriousness of what was happening. They did not imagine that they would not be permitted to return to their homes and property. Among the people who remained, very few had guns (including my father, who did not believe in having guns), and they had no training on how to use them. The Palestinians could not believe that the Zionists would be able to take over Palestine. After all, the Palestinians were the indigenous people of the land and the majority population. In those days there were no TVs, and many families had no radio. Some Palestinians were terrified of the Zionists because of what they had done in the village of Deir Yassin on the outskirts of Jerusalem. Zionists had occupied the village and massacred

1. I am thankful to my sister Neda who kept a diary about our expulsion from Beisan. Some of the included details in this section come from her diary.

3

over a hundred Palestinian men, women, and children, and paraded some of the victims in the streets of Jerusalem.

The Zionists were the minority, and it did not make sense that the minority would be capable of overtaking the majority. The fact is, however, that the Zionists were much better trained and equipped to fight and they were much more prepared than the Palestinians. Some of them fought alongside the British army in WWII, and Britain was supportive of the Zionist takeover.

On November 2, 1917, before Britain had a mandate over Palestine, the British government had issued the Balfour Declaration[2] in which it promised the Zionists a homeland in Palestine for the Jewish people. Britain did not own Palestine and had no authority to give the land to other people. It was done within the framework and spirit of colonialism and imperialism of the time. Since the end of WWI, when Britain was given the mandate over Palestine, the Zionist Jewish leadership was preparing themselves through meticulous organization and planning as well as by encouraging the immigration of Jews into Palestine through legal and illegal means, to beef up the Jewish population of the land. The Zionists were much better organized militarily and politically than the Palestinians.

It is important to add another dimension. In 1947, the United Nations partitioned Palestine against the will of the majority of its people. According to the Partition Plan, the Jewish people were given approximately 57 percent of the land of Palestine while they owned less than 6 percent of the land and constituted a minority of the population. The Palestinians, the indigenous people of the land, who were the majority of the population and owned over 90 percent of the land, were given just 43 percent.[3] The Palestinians rejected the Partition Plan as unjust, while the Zionist leadership accepted it. It was against the principle of self-determination, which the great powers of the time refused to grant the Palestinians. It was only then, and for the first time, that Jewish people could claim any legal right to the

2. See "Balfour Declaration." The Balfour Declaration was a public statement issued by the British government in 1917 during the First World War announcing support for the establishment of a "national home for the Jewish people" in Palestine, then an Ottoman region with a small minority Jewish population. It read: "His Majesty's Government view with favour the establishment in Palestine of a national home for the Jewish people and will use their best endeavours to facilitate the achievement of this object, it being clearly understood that nothing shall be done which may prejudice the civil and religious rights of existing non-Jewish communities in Palestine, or the rights and political status enjoyed by Jews in any other country."

3. Sayegh, *Time Bomb*, 51.

land, though it was won and achieved in violation of international law, and through much intrigue, deception, and bribery. What is even more telling is that when the Zionist militias started militarily to claim the 57 percent of the land that was granted to them by the UN, they were so successful that they were not satisfied by conquering the 57 percent; they kept pushing the Palestinians out. When they stopped, they had taken over 78 percent of the land of Palestine and refused to return to their allotted share. Approximately 750,000 Palestinians were dispossessed and ethnically cleansed and over five hundred villages and towns were demolished or depopulated. A mere 150,000 Palestinians remained within that area of Palestine, which became Israel, many having been displaced from their homes. In the war of 1967, Israel conquered the remaining 22 percent (the West Bank, including East Jerusalem, and the Gaza Strip), thus controlling the whole land of Palestine.[4]

I was playing outside our house in Beisan watching the Zionist soldiers march through our town. There was no resistance. Beisan was simply taken over. Zionist soldiers came into peoples' houses looking for guns. They came into our house and my father told them that we did not have any guns. For two weeks we lived under Zionist Jewish rule. I watched the looting of Palestinian homes. Trucks came empty and left full of furniture and anything else of value, including Persian rugs and food supplies. The shops of Beisan were full of goods and merchandise; all were emptied by the Zionists.

According to our church's register, on Sunday, May 16, 1948, my father held a morning prayer service at the Church of the Good Shepherd in Beisan after the occupation. It was Pentecost Sunday. There is no record of how many people attended church that Sunday, but my father preached on Acts 2:4, "All of them were filled with the Holy Spirit and began to speak in other languages, as the Spirit gave them ability." The following Sunday was Trinity Sunday, May 23. Again, my father held the morning prayer service at 9:30 a.m. with people of Beisan attending. The following Wednesday, May 26, the Zionist governor summoned the heads of the churches and the Muslim community. (My father was summoned because he was the point person for the Protestant church.) They went to the headquarters at the Beisan Tegart[5] building. The governor told them that they had two hours

4. Sayegh, *Time Bomb*, 51.

5. A Tegart is a type of militarized police fort constructed throughout Palestine during the British Mandatory period.

to evacuate the town, and those who didn't leave would be killed. My father pleaded with the governor: "I have nowhere to go. This is our home. I have a large family. Let us stay and live in our town." I still remember my father's words, but the governor's answer was loud and clear: "If you don't leave, we will kill you." This is what my father told us when he came back from that meeting. Then he said, we have been asked to meet at the Saraya,[6] the government headquarters, in the center of town. My father asked us to take whatever was light but of value. It was a frantic and chaotic time. What can you take of importance from your home? My sister Neda had just baked fresh bread. This was important.

We did not know where we would be going. Mother gave us things to take and told us to take them to the Saraya and then come back to take more. So, Naomi and I carried what we were given and went. When we got there, we found that the Zionist soldiers had encircled the whole downtown area. They asked us, "Are you Muslim or Christian?" We said, "Christian." They pointed us to an area and told us to go there. When I wanted to return home, a soldier pointed the rifle in my face and ordered me to stay. The same thing happened to my sisters. Eventually, all of us came and were trapped inside the area, the Muslims on one side and the Christians on the other.

One of our neighbors was a Muslim. He came to my father and told him, "I want to go where you go." So, his family pretended they were Christians and stood with us. It's amazing that after over seventy years, I still remember those moments, and how the soldier pointed his rifle in my face and would not let me go back home.

Uncle Suleiman Ateek and his fourteen-year-old daughter brought some things from their home and left their youngest two daughters, six and eight years old, at home thinking he would be back to get them. But the soldiers would not let him go back. He and his daughter were shouting and crying. People were overwhelmed by all types of emotions—fear, anger, bitterness, desire for revenge, helplessness, hopelessness, and every other human feeling. Eventually, they allowed my uncle to go bring his daughters.

My mother was still at home waiting for us. She was very anxious and worried about whatever might have happened to us. Some Jewish soldiers passed by and asked her why she was still there. She told them, "I am waiting for my children to return." They told her that they would not return,

---

6. Turkish for government building that was considered to have particular administrative importance in various parts of the former Ottoman Empire.

that she needed to hurry up and go to meet them at the town center. She carried what she could and came to the Saraya.

When mother arrived, we were all standing there not knowing what would happen. Would they force us to walk out of town or would they bring some buses? We explained to mother what happened to us. Suddenly mother remembered that she left her purse in the basket in front of our house and in it fifty Palestinian pounds. In those days fifty pounds was a large sum of money. At the same time, Michel remembered that he forgot his small Philips radio that he treasured very much. In those days, to have a radio was extremely important in order to hear the news and to know what was happening in the country.

The Zionist militias ordered the Muslims to start walking toward the Jordan River, east of Beisan to the country of Jordan, and the Christians to go to Nazareth. The Zionists then brought buses to transport us to Nazareth. Since the bus had to pass in front of our house, Michel pleaded with the driver to stop the bus for a minute to bring some powdered milk for his baby. Quickly, Michel was able to place the basket with my mother's purse on the bus. He also went to his room and placed his radio inside a mattress and brought it on the bus. My father and brother were able to smuggle out the gold but could not take the silver. In fact, they dug out a hole in our garden and placed in it a big box of all the silver ornaments that they had made. Everything else was left behind. The buses that were carrying the Christians went as far as the outskirts of Nazareth, which was still not occupied by the Jewish Zionist militias. They literally dumped us there. It took a few hours before the word got to Nazareth that the people of Beisan had been forced out. Buses and cars then came to take us into Nazareth.

Everything that my father had built and worked for, the three houses he built, the business he established during the previous twenty-five years, not to mention the church he loved and helped build, the beautiful life of Beisan where all of us children were born, the garden we enjoyed with all its fruit trees and delicious fruits, were all lost by a Zionist decision to ethnically cleanse Beisan of its six thousand Palestinian inhabitants.

Before we were expelled, the Zionist military governor told the heads of the religious communities of Beisan that our displacement would be temporary. We were told that it would only be for two weeks, and then we would be able to return. Such a statement must have been a deceptive trick used by the Zionists not only in Beisan but in other places. We know it was used when the people of Iqrit and Kufur Berem[7] were evicted.

What happened to Beisan happened to many towns and villages. As mentioned, by the end of the war, approximately three quarters of a million Palestinians, men, women, and children, were displaced and dispossessed. In order to prevent them from returning home, the Israeli military demolished close to five hundred villages and towns throughout Palestine. Beisan was not demolished. They made it the temporary home for thousands of Jewish refugees they had brought from north Africa. They changed its name from Beisan to its biblical name, Beit Shean.

At Christmas in 1948, the *New York Times* published an article by George Barrett, "The Star of Bethlehem Looks Down on 750,000 Refugees in Holy Land—That Is, Report of U.N. Children's Emergency Fund, Which Says Many Who Lost Homes in War Are Sleeping in Stables."[8] This was the first Christmas after the Nakba (catastrophe) of 1948.

May 15, 1948, will remain indelibly ingrained in the memory of Palestinians and their offspring as the darkest day of the twentieth century. It was Al-Nakba Day. But that day is only symbolic of the catastrophe that struck the Palestinians before and after that date. In fact, the Nakba started with UN Resolution 181 on November 29, 1947, with the Partition Plan of Palestine. For our family, the Nakba began on May 26, 1948, when we were forced out at gunpoint by the Zionist militias from our home and town. The Nakba turned the life of over 1.3 million Palestinians upside down. For most Palestinians, it was the brutal uprooting from their homes, properties, and lands, and collectively, the loss of their homeland.

In their long history, the people of Palestine had experienced many foreign occupations of their homeland, but, by and large, the people stayed on their land. There has always been a special connection between the people and the land. The Zionists believed that by breaking this bond and throwing them out, the Palestinians would forget Palestine. This did not happen. What continues to be amazing is the mental, emotional, psychological, and spiritual resilience of the Palestinians and their strong attachment to Palestine. It has been over seventy years since the Nakba, and the Palestinians refuse to forget or give up on their rights. Although we realize that we are up against a stubborn settler colonial Zionist ideology,

---

7. Iqrit and Kufur Berem were two Christian villages in the north of Palestine that were forcefully depopulated. For details, see Chacour, *Blood Brothers.*

8. Barrett, "Star of Bethlehem."

the indigenous Palestinians will continue to pursue the struggle for justice until the international community renders them the justice and peace they are entitled to.

The love of Palestine is being passed on from one generation to another to wherever the Palestinian dispersion and diaspora has taken them, whether in other parts of the Middle East or across the whole world. Many of them are still living in camps in Jordan, Lebanon, and Syria, and they long to return to Palestine.

I was eleven years old when the Nakba struck, but I still remember some intricate details, and I relish many fond memories of Beisan. The well-known Lebanese singer, Fairouz, has a lovely song about Beisan. She sings, "Long ago, we had an orchard and a winter house in Beisan. Take me to Beisan, my childhood playground, my memories, our house, its door, its windows. Take me to Beisan. Many people are longing and weeping to return to Beisan. Take me to Beisan."[9]

9. Fairuz, "Bissan."

2

Life Before the Nakba

My father, Stifan Salameh Ateek, was born in a devout Eastern Ortho-dox Christian family in Nablus,[1] Palestine, in 1892. The Christian commu-nity in Nablus has deep historical roots going back to the ministry of Philip, one of the seven deacons chosen by the early church according to the book of Acts, chapters 6 and 8.

In 1966, I visited Nablus with Bishop Najib Cub'ain. During my visit, I met the head of the Samaritan community, Kahin Omran. To my pleasant surprise, he was a classmate of my father. In our conversation, he asked me whether I knew why our family's name is Ateek. I said no. Then, he looked me in the eye and explained to me that it was "because you were one of the oldest Christian families in Nablus, you were called Ateek." Ateek means old or antique. I don't recall that my father had ever mentioned this to me. But I liked his answer. Obviously, I have no way of verifying or authenticat-ing such a wonderful claim, but his answer was sumptuous. It was amazing; I started using it.

My grandfather Salameh Salman Ateek was born in Nablus and worked as a cobbler. He married Hanneh Aghabi, also from Nablus, and God blessed them with four children, two boys and two girls. The oldest was my father. He was born on St. Stephen's Day, December 26, 1892, so

---

1. Shechem in the Bible. It was named Neapolis by Roman emperor Vespasian, and the Arabs called it Nablus. It is approximately 50 kilometers (30 miles) north of Jerusalem and is one of the two largest cities in Palestine. It is famous for its Arabic sweet, Kenafeh.

they named him Stifan, which is Arabic for Stephen. Then came a girl. They named her Azeezeh, which means "dear and precious." Then came another boy, and they named him Mikhael after the Archangel Michael. The youngest was Mariam. While still in Nablus, tragedy struck.

My uncle Mikhael was a good-looking young man but energetic and "wild." One day he was friendly wrestling with one of his friends and the two managed to fall on the ground on top of each other. Mikhael's silver cigarette box was in his shirt pocket. When he landed over his friend, the silver box pressed on his lungs. It must have broken some ribs and caused internal bleeding. A few days later, May 28, 1916, he died. He was twenty-two years old.

Less than two years later, on March 18, 1918, my grandmother Hanneh died of asthma. She was fifty-five years old. It was left to my father and his two sisters to care for their father Salameh. A few years later, when my father left Nablus and went to settle in Beisan, my grandfather was there with him. My mother was his main caretaker until his death.

Another tragic story befell my Aunt Azeezeh. She married Boulos Mazzawi from Nazareth and they lived together for three years. She gave birth to a daughter who died in infancy. Her husband then fell sick, and his health started to deteriorate and after a few months he died. Azeezeh left Nazareth and went to Beisan to live close to her brother. Later, my father built her an apartment on our land, close to our home.

Aunt Mariam married George Kharouba, a friend of my father from Nablus. In fact, both learned the profession of goldsmith and jeweler. Later, George and Mariam moved to the town of Jenin (27 kilometers/17 miles north of Nablus). He was one of the first goldsmiths in town and had a very successful business career. George and Mariam did not have children and after George's death, Aunt Mariam stayed in Jenin among many friends and relatives.

Mariam was a very devout Christian. Although she was brought up in the Eastern Orthodox Church, during her life, and especially after the death of her husband, she worshiped God wherever it was possible and convenient. In Jenin, the Christian community was small and there was no resident Orthodox priest, but there was a resident Latin (Roman Catholic) priest. So, she attended the Latin church regularly and learned its liturgy as well as her own. Moreover, due to her regular visits with us, she became acquainted with the Anglican liturgy. I remember with great fondness the many times both of us would spend singing hymns from the three Christian traditions of our land. She had an amazing memory and knew the words of many hymns and chants by heart. In fact, she taught me a few Orthodox and Catholic hymns. She introduced me to Father Manuel Musallam, the Latin priest in Jenin, and over time we became very good friends. He later spent many years as the priest of the Latin parish in Gaza and, in that capacity, he served not only the small Christian community in Gaza but the Muslim community as well. Due to tough times in Gaza, years later when Sabeel came into being, we used to collect and send money through Abuna (Father) Manuel for the poor and needy in Gaza.

Infrequently, I would choose to pass through Jenin on my way to Jerusalem for meetings. I would leave Haifa in the afternoon and spend the night with Aunt Mariam and enjoy an evening visit with Abuna Manuel. Our relationship with one another was cemented due to the generous hospitality of my aunt.

Aunt Mariam lived for over fifty years in the same rented house from the Haddad family in Jenin. The time came when her wonderful neighbors moved across town and built the Haddad Village, which became a recreation center for Jenin and for all the West Bank. Later, her brother-in-law and his family left Jenin and moved to Zababdeh. She was already in her eighties and with the deteriorating political situation and the difficulties of movement between Israel and the West Bank, I became more concerned about her health and safety. I decided to arrange for her to move to Ebenezer Home in Haifa, close to St. John's Church where I was serving.

My father was brought up in Nablus. He attended the mission school that had been established by The Church Missionary Society (CMS).[2] The CMS missionaries had started their work in Palestine, including Jordan, in the 1850s, when Bishop Samuel Gobat became bishop in Jerusalem. They built schools and hospitals and established mission stations all over Palestine, which, at that time, was still part of the Ottoman Empire. At one point they had over fifty schools scattered around the country.

They built a hospital and the school in Nablus that my father attended. In those days, the schools were rudimentary, but they gave the children basic education in reading, writing, and math. I believe he finished the fourth grade. As was the case in missionary schools, the children were taught the Bible and learned Protestant hymns and prayers. They had daily

2. The Church Missionary Society (CMS) is a British mission society working with the Anglican communion and Protestant Christians around the world. Founded in 1799, CMS has attracted over nine thousand men and women to serve as mission partners during its two-hundred-year history.

chapel services. Father was a keen student, and his religious studies and daily prayers awakened and stimulated his Christian faith. Although he kept his connection with the Orthodox church, he gravitated toward the "Protestant" missionaries' ministry where his knowledge of the Bible, and especially of the gospels, strengthened and deepened his faith.[3]

The missionaries were also conducting regular meetings of Bible study for the community. This was a new phenomenon for the Nablus Christians. The missionaries had brought with them small harmoniums, pump organs, that were used to lead and accompany the singing. People from the Nablus Christian community and even a few Muslims would gather at the mission house, and the missionaries would teach them Christian songs. They would read a portion from the Bible and elaborate on it, and they would pray together. This was basically the simple format that was followed. For Orthodox Christians, who were used to hearing the gospel being chanted in church (sometimes in Greek), seldom having anyone to explain it to them, it was a breath of fresh air. An increasing number of Christians started attending these services. Some local Christians, inevitably, were drawn in and began to associate with the missionaries. For them, it was not a new gospel; it was a more simplified and clarified gospel, as if someone had stripped the outside coating and focused on the heart of the Christian faith. Some Christians became regular in their attendance and eventually joined this new Protestant church. My father was one of those young men who was influenced by the teaching of the missionaries. There were others who were attracted to the missionaries because of the healing ministry that the hospital was providing to the people of Nablus and its vicinity.

My father's life was changed during this time. His Christian faith was deepened through the study of the Bible and especially the New Testament. He decided to let his faith impact all aspects of his life, including his business and family life. Years later, he wrote an article in the church magazine, entitled "Christ in the Shop of a Goldsmith," in which he related how, through the study of the gospels, he had decided to take his faith seriously and to live out his faith in his daily life and business.

Father felt indebted to the missionaries for bringing the evangelical and Protestant perspective of faith to Palestine. Through opening the Bible and explaining and interpreting its spiritual riches, they helped many people to discover and to meet Jesus Christ in a more personal way.

3. The Protestant Church was a general designation given to all those local Arab Christians who joined the Protestant missions. It distinguished them from the Orthodox or Catholic Christians.

Father worked for some time at the mission hospital in Nablus, one of the first hospitals, if not the first, to be established in the city. He later left the hospital and started training to become a goldsmith. It is important to note that the nephew of the owner of the goldsmith shop where my father was training was Fayek Durzi (later Haddad) who years later became an Anglican minister. In 1976, he became the first Arab Palestinian Anglican Bishop in Jerusalem.[4]

Sometime after 1910, my father was drafted by the Turkish army and sent to Istanbul for military training. The journey was dangerous and treacherous. As a boy I used to hear older people talk about the infamous "Safar Barlik,"[5] the journey by land to Istanbul that many young people were forced to make, and where some died on the way. Father arrived in Istanbul very sick and spent several weeks in the hospital. After his release he was permitted to return to Nablus for a year of convalescence. While in Nablus, he continued his training to become a goldsmith. In 1914, when the First World War started, like many Arabs of Palestine, he did not want to join the Turkish army and decided to hide out. The Arabs throughout the region of the Middle East were hoping to see the defeat of the Ottoman Empire and the end of four hundred years of its decadent rule and occupation. Father, therefore, decided to leave Nablus and go down to the Jordan valley to hide out among the Bedouin tribes there. Over twenty Bedouin tribes lived in the Beisan area. He was hoping that some of them would welcome him. The Bedouins, like the rest of the Arabs, were anxious to see the toppling of the Ottoman Empire, and my father found refuge there for the next four years of the war. One of the most interesting incidents my Aunt Mariam related to me was when some Turkish soldiers came looking for "deserters." Some of my father's Bedouin friends were worried about his safety, and since he was under their protection, they had to come up with a watertight solution even if it was bizarre and culturally unthinkable. They made him put on

---

4. Bishop Haddad was preceded by Bishop Najib Cub'ain, the first Arab to be consecrated as bishop of the diocese of Jordan, Lebanon, and Syria, which was later incorporated within "The Jerusalem Bishopric of the Episcopal Church in Jerusalem and the Middle East."

5. The Ottoman term Safar Barlik referred to the mobilization effected by the late Ottoman Empire during the Second Balkan War of 1913 and World War I from 1914 to 1918, which involved the forced conscription of Syrian, including Palestinian, men to fight on its behalf and deportation of numerous Syrian families to Anatolia under Djemal Pasha's orders.

a Bedouin woman's dress and stay within the women's quarters so that he would not be discovered. It worked.

In 1918, the war ended with the defeat of the Axis powers, including Turkey. This resulted in the disintegration of the Turkish Empire. The Ottoman provinces were divided between Britain and France. The British army under the leadership of General Allenby had already occupied Palestine and East Jordan. After the war ended, my father returned to Nablus where he completed his training and began work as a goldsmith.

Through the help of some friends from Nablus, my father's marriage was arranged to a young girl from Tulkarem, a small town a few kilometers west of Nablus. The girl's name was Nawart Karnik Sarkisian. On June 20, 1921, Stifan and Nawart were married in St. Philip's Anglican Church in Nablus by the late Rev. Elias Marmura. My father Stifan was twenty-nine years old and Nawart was fourteen. The big difference in age was not unusual in those days.

The story of the Sarkisian family began when my mother Nawart's father, Karnik Sarkisian, an Armenian Turkish government employee, was commissioned to leave Istanbul and travel to Palestine and head its telegraph office in Beersheba. In those days, the telegraph was the best system of communication, and it was important to be managed responsibly and efficiently.

In the late nineteenth and early twentieth centuries, Beersheba was the center for the large Bedouin tribes in that region and throughout the Negev. There were very few Christians living in Beersheba at the time. Almost all the population within the wide-ranging Bedouin tribes that inhabited the Negev region was Muslim.[6]

Beersheba was primarily a Bedouin town and was not conducive to urban city life. It was natural for my grandfather Karnik, a young man in his thirties, to look for a Christian community where he could cultivate friendships and enjoy some social life. The closest place for that was the city of Gaza, approximately 42 kilometers (26 miles) away where the Christian community was numerous and quite vibrant. Moreover, it was one of the oldest Christian communities in Palestine. Gaza is mentioned in the book of Acts chapter 8 in the story of Philip the deacon and the conversion of the

---

6. At the time of the 1922 census of Palestine (see "1922 Census"), Beersheba had a population of 2,012 Muslims, 235 Christians, 98 Jews, and 11 Druze (total 2,356). At the time of the 1931 census (see "1931 Census"), Beersheba had 545 occupied houses and a population of 2,791 Muslims, 152 Christians, 11 Jews, and 5 Bahá'í (total 2,959). The 1945 village survey conducted by the Palestine Mandate government found 5,360 Muslims, 200 Christians, and 10 others (total 5,570).

Ethiopian eunuch. In addition, there was a strong Christian tradition that, in early centuries, a number of saints lived in Gaza.[7]

Unfortunately, my information about my maternal grandfather is sparse. I can, however, surmise that Grandfather Karnik must have felt very lonely in Beersheba, away from his parents and family life in Istanbul, the large and beautiful capital of the Turkish Empire. More than once, mother told me that the Sarkisian family was well-to-do. She remembered her father saying that their family home in Istanbul was not very far from the residence of the Turkish Sultan. Be that as it may, we know that my grandfather Karnik used to go to visit Gaza whenever his job permitted it.

The Christian community of Gaza had deep historical roots and constituted the elite families in the city.[8] The Christian families were all members of the Orthodox Church where there was a resident priest, and so it was easy for my grandfather Karnik to make friends there. One of those established and well-to-do families was the Farah family. Grandfather Karnik had met Boulos Farah since he was his counterpart in Gaza working at the telegraph office there. Mr. Farah befriended Karnik and invited him to his home, in line with Arab hospitality. Through the Farah family, my grandfather met a number of the Christians of Gaza and felt welcomed by their friendship and warmth.

The Farah family had three daughters. My grandfather was attracted to Katrina, the oldest. In due time, they were married in the Orthodox Church in Gaza. God blessed them with four children, three girls and one boy, Margaret, Mariam, Kamel, and Nawart. My mother, Nawart, was the youngest. She was born in 1906 in Beirut and was baptized in the Armenian Orthodox Church there, when my grandfather was transferred to Lebanon for several months. My mother was given a beautiful Armenian name, Nevart, which means "rosebud," but because the Arabic language does not have a "v" sound, everyone called her Nawart. Tragically, however, when Nawart was only a few years old, her father died of a urinary tract infection. He was just fifty-five years old, and his death left Katrina with four small children. The family stayed in Gaza for a while longer and

---

7. According to tradition, a number of saints have been connected with Gaza: St. Porphyrius was bishop of Gaza in the fourth century; St. Dorotheus, a monk and abbot in the sixth century; and St. Vitalis of Gaza was a hermit in the seventh century.

8. The CMS missionaries had built a hospital to serve the people of Gaza and its vicinity. This hospital was the predecessor of Ahli Arab Hospital, now administered by the Anglican diocese of Jerusalem. Ahli played an important part in Gaza's history, especially during the first intifada, as the only independent (nongovernment) hospital in Gaza.

then Grandmother Katrina decided to move to Tulkarem.[9] With the help of friends, she placed her two oldest daughters, Maggie and Mariam, at the Schneller boarding school in Jerusalem, leaving the two youngest children, Kamel and Nawart, with her at home. Relatively speaking, Tulkarem was closer to Jerusalem and the public transportation was easier to Schneller. I remember my mother telling me that she was six years old when the family left Gaza, probably due to the deteriorating political situation and the impending start of WWI.

Tulkarem was a small town with a small Christian community living in the midst of a much larger Muslim population. There was an Eastern Orthodox church in the town but no resident priest. The priest came from Nablus on Sundays to celebrate the Divine Liturgy.

After Maggie and Mariam completed their education at Schneller school in Jerusalem,[10] Maggie was trained as an assistant pharmacist. She worked for the Ministry of Health in Tulkarem and later worked as the housekeeper at the Baptist Hospital in Ajloon, Jordan. When she retired, she lived with my Uncle Kamel and his family in Ramallah until her death in 1964.

Aunt Mariam got married and lived in Jerusalem, but we have no information about her married life. What we know is that she remained in Jerusalem and worked with German families as a housemother. Because of her education and life at Schneller, Aunt Mariam's German and English proficiency was much better than her Arabic. After she retired, she remained living in the German colony in Jerusalem. She worshiped regularly at St. Andrew's Church of Scotland close by. Thankfully, with the help of her friends, we were able to find a place for her at Ebenezer Home in Haifa.

9. Tulkarem is a Palestinian city with a population of 51,000 approximately 23 miles northwest of Nablus.

10. Schneller Orphanage was a German Protestant orphanage established by Johann Ludwig Schneller (1820–96), a German Lutheran missionary, which operated in Jerusalem from 1860 to 1940. It was one of the first structures to be built outside the Old City of Jerusalem. In 1860, Lebanese Druze massacred thousands of Maronite Christians in Lebanon and Syria. Schneller travelled to Beirut with the intention of rescuing battle-orphaned children. He was rebuffed by the local community, which did not trust foreign Protestant missionaries, but managed to bring back nine orphaned boys to Jerusalem in October 1860. He decided to open an orphanage for them in his home, and by the end of 1861 had enrolled forty-one boys in what became known as the Syrian Orphanage. The school was known for its strict upbringing. The children were more German than Palestinian. They had very good schooling and learned various trades and the men became very successful in their various professions, especially carpentry, blacksmithing, and others. For many years, most of the organists in our Lutheran and Anglican churches were graduates of the Schneller schools.

Several years later, I was able to arrange for Aunt Mariam from my father's side to come to Ebenezer Home in Haifa as well. I was thankful that both of my aunts Mariam, from my mother's and father's side, had been accepted to spend their last years well taken care of by wonderful local and international Christian workers at Ebenezer.

Ebenezer Home was built to accommodate European messianic Jews, i.e., Jews who had accepted Jesus as their Messiah, some of whom had survived the Holocaust and been brought to Israel through the help of the Norwegian Mission. Due to my friendly relationship with the Norwegian pastor, the mission agreed to admit a few local Christians to the home, especially those who had spent years in Christian service. That opened the door for a handful of Christian Arab members to be accepted at Ebenezer. That agreement has continued until today.

For the first few years, the two Mariams did not get along with one another. For all practical purposes, Mariam Sarkisian was culturally German in both language and way of life, while Mariam Ateek was culturally Palestinian Arab. It was difficult and painful to observe this, but we could not change the situation. Thankfully, each had her own room on a different floor. I always felt that my Aunt Mariam Sarkisian was the more difficult in temperament. But one day a miracle happened. My Aunt Mariam Sarkisian got sick and became bedridden. Aunt Mariam Ateek visited her, looked after her, and showed her kindness and love. From then on, they became the best of friends.

A few years after I moved from Haifa to serve the church at St. George's Cathedral in Jerusalem, the phone rang one day, and the voice said, "Assis Naim, your Aunt Mariam died, please come." I asked, "which Mariam?" She said, "I don't know." If we were speaking in Arabic, there wouldn't be a confusion. In Arabic, there is a different word for the aunt of the father's side and the mother's side, but not so in English. It was Aunt Mariam Ateek who died at age ninety-four on August 5, 1994. My Aunt Mariam Sarkisian lived a few more years before she passed away. Both were buried in our church's cemetery in Haifa. And both went to be with the Lord.

Uncle Kamel grew up to be a very handsome young man. He worked in Tulkarem in the shoe business and eventually had his own shoe shop. He married a beautiful young woman from the Jarjoura family of Nazareth and God blessed them with five girls and three boys. Grandmother Katrina encouraged Kamel to give the male children names of animals of prey. She mentioned that in two different pregnancies she had given birth to boys, but both died in infancy. She believed that had their names been those of animals, they could have survived. My uncle did not want to argue with his mother about such superstitions, and out of respect for her, he agreed to do it. They already had two girls, Rose and Lily, so my uncle continued to give the girls names of flowers, Violet, Yasmine (Jasmin), and Sawsan (Lily of the Valley), and gave the boys names of animals, namely, Sabi', Nimer, and Fahad—Lion, Tiger, and Leopard, respectively. These names were not in any way unique and exceptional; they are still popular names for male children in the Palestinian community.

I am especially proud of my cousin Sabi', the oldest of my uncle's sons. He became an Anglican (Episcopal) minister and served mainly the church in Azzarqa, Jordan. He occupied several positions in the church council of the Jerusalem Diocese of the Episcopal Church and was made an honorary Canon of St. George's Cathedral. After his retirement, he and his family moved to the United States and settled down in the St. Louis area. Canon Sabi' passed away on Orthodox Good Friday, April 17, 2020, in St. Louis, Missouri. The funeral was held on Orthodox Easter Sunday. Due to the coronavirus pandemic, I officiated at his funeral online from Texas, using the Arabic liturgy, with only his immediate family present. He was buried in Chicago.

In 1950, my uncle Kamel left Tulkarem and moved with his wife, children, and his mother Katrina to Ramallah. In Ramallah, he bought a piece of land on which he built a nice house and settled there. Uncle Kamel was a dedicated Christian and he and his wife Najla brought up the children in the love of the Lord. When they were living in Tulkarem, my uncle used to hold Christian services in his home to deepen the faith of the Christian community in town. He also served as a treasurer for the Orthodox Church there. When the family moved to Ramallah in 1950, he became active at St. Andrew's Episcopal Church. For thirty-five years he looked after the finances of the church voluntarily. When he did the financial report at the end of the year, he would always add ten Jordanian dinars to ensure that he did not, unwittingly, make a mistake.

In 1962, Grandmother Katrina died in Ramallah. She was eighty-six years old. My uncle continued his life of faith, serving the church and community in Ramallah. On April 1, 1991, he went to be with the Lord. He was ninety years old.

As I look back at the early history of our family, I am amazed at the passage of time and the movement of people and events. Total strangers met and became family, and their children grew up and were intimately interconnected with others. New families and communities were formed. Faith in God and love of Christ were nurtured by others from foreign lands. People's lives were changed for the better.

For many people, it is the natural way of human life, the web of life. There is no overall purpose or design. However, when I look at it from the perspective of my faith, I see God's hand guiding and leading individuals and families, creating, connecting, and blessing people and their pedigrees.

Thus began the journey through life of Stifan and Nawart Ateek. Her father came from Istanbul, Turkey; my father was from Nablus, Palestine. They married in Nablus and God blessed them with a large family in Beisan. They did not journey through life alone. Christ was leading them, even going with them through the valley of the shadow of death during the Nakba and into "refugee-dom."

3

My Life in Beisan

THE TOWN OF BEISAN is situated in the Jordan Valley. In the winter months, the weather is very pleasant, while the summer is very hot. It has a rich history going back to more than three thousand years before Christ, to the times of the ancient Canaanite tribes that inhabited the region. In those years, the ancient Egyptians controlled and governed it. Behind our house was the Tel (mound) that had been partly excavated when we were still living there, and I remember as a boy visiting the place with my family and even playing there with my sisters.

Over its long history, it has been known by several names—Beit Shean, or Beit Shan, Scythopolis, and Beisan. At the time of Jesus, it was known as Scythopolis and was the capital of the Decapolis cities (ten cities) we read about in the gospels. In the early Christian centuries, there was a sizable Christian community in Beisan, and its bishop attended the Council of Nicea in AD 325. Relatively close to Beisan, on the other side of the Jordan River, lies Pella (Tabaqat Fahle), another Decapolis city. According to Christian tradition, the early followers of Jesus Christ fled Jerusalem to Pella during the siege of Jerusalem before AD 70 when Jerusalem was destroyed by the Romans. To the east of Beisan is the Jordan River, about five kilometers away (less than three miles). Once you cross the river, you are in the country of Jordan. Around Beisan were over twenty-two Arab Palestinian Bedouin villages, and since Beisan was the region's small capital city of around six thousand inhabitants, most of the villagers came to do their trading, shopping, and conduct their business in Beisan. All the villages were destroyed by Israel after 1948.

After their marriage, my father and mother continued to live in Nablus for a few years and gave birth to their first two children, Michel (Michael) and Hanneh. Michel was born on April 26, 1923. He was named after my father's brother, uncle Mikhael, who died when he was a young man. My mother was sixteen when Michel was born. Next, Hanneh (Ann) was born on July 21, 1924, and was named after my grandmother, who had died several years before.

Sometime later, my father and mother and their young family left Nablus and moved to Beisan, taking my grandfather Salameh with them. They rented a small house, and my father started his goldsmith business. He was aware that he had two different clienteles. The town dwellers of Beisan liked to buy gold jewelry while the Bedouin villagers around Beisan preferred silver. He had to cater to both.

My Father

Since father took his Christian faith seriously, he tried to practice his faith in both his home and business. His prices were fixed, his profit was reasonable, and he rejected the customary business practices, including any haggling or bargaining. He refrained from swearing or using unethical ways. In addition, he decided to give a tithe of his income to God. In order to facilitate this practice, he set a special box on the side, designated it "For the Lord" and placed in it the tithe, a tenth of every item he sold. Before long, God's money started to multiply. He used it to help the poor people in Beisan and especially the Christians. His motto was, "Do good to all, especially for the family of faith" (Gal 6:10). On feast days it became a practice to help needy people in Beisan. He never looked for publicity or fame. He believed that he was obedient to the teaching of Christ in the Gospel of Matthew: "if you do it to one of the least of my brethren you do it to me" (Matt 25:40).

After a difficult illness that sent him to the "English" hospital in Nazareth, he made an agreement with the hospital administration to pay the expenses of one bed at the hospital for any needy sick person who could not afford the treatment. On feast days, he would send food supplies to poor families. In those days the basic staples were flour, rice, and sugar.

My grandfather Salameh lived in Beisan as a revered member of our family, and my siblings enjoyed having their grandfather around. On April

17, 1930, my grandfather Salameh died and was buried in Beisan. I still remember how my mother described his last day before his death. It was Maundy Thursday, according to the Eastern calendar, when Christians celebrate Jesus' institution of the Lord's Supper, the Holy Communion, with his disciples in Jerusalem. That afternoon, my grandfather took a bath, got dressed in his traditional Arab *qumbaz*,[1] and with my father walked to the Orthodox church to attend the Maundy Thursday Divine Liturgy. My father participated in the chants and singing of the liturgy as he was accustomed to do. When the time came for receiving the sacrament, they both received communion and returned home. That night, grandfather Salameh went to sleep, and went to be with the Lord. He was eighty years old. My mother always said that he was a devoutly pious man.

As my father's business flourished and expanded, he was able to buy a piece of land of two and a half dunums (more than half an acre). The land was situated on the main street that crossed Beisan. The Eastern Orthodox Church was right across the street from our land, and further up to the south was the Latin (Roman Catholic) Church. Next to our land, on the eastern side, was the town's elementary school.

In the early 1930s, father was financially able to construct a big house on the land for his expanding family. He later built a multipurpose hall that he could use for Sunday school, Bible study, and Sunday worship and any other function in the service of the Lord. He used to hold regular meetings to teach and instruct the Christian community of Beisan about the meaning of faith and love of God. The format was simple—singing hymns, a reading from the Bible, interpreting and preaching the word of God, and prayer. For singing, he used his small diatonic accordion. Later, he was able to acquire a small pump organ, which the CMS missionaries provided.

On Sundays, this hall was used for worship. The attendees were a small group of Orthodox and Catholic Christians who enjoyed this simple Protestant service where everyone could join in through a simple liturgy they could easily understand and participate in. Before too long, a small community of Protestant Christians was formed. Once a month, an ordained minister came from Nazareth to celebrate the Holy Communion. On the other Sundays of the month, one of the laymen from the emerging church congregation led the people in morning or evening prayer and preached a

---

1. *Qumbaz* used to be the traditional men's wear. During the British Mandate, many Palestinians replaced the *Qumbaz* with Western pants. My father never did. He continued to wear the *Qumbaz* with a jacket and a fez on his head.

sermon. My father was one of three laymen who officiated in the absence of a minister. The relationship between this nascent Protestant community and the Orthodox church was good. At times, some of the Orthodox Christians would attend the Protestant service. They enjoyed singing the hymns and listening to the sermon, which was not available in their own church.[2]

The small community of believers, originally Orthodox or Catholics, began to think, pray, and dream of someday building a church in Beisan. To accelerate the process of building a church, my father was able, with the help of CMS, the Majma (local church council of the Anglican Church), and other donations, to buy a small plot of land near the Catholic Church where a future Anglican Church would be built. In the meantime, the hall my father had built could be used. In fact, on March 21, 1936, Bishop George Francis Graham Brown, Anglican Bishop in Jerusalem, accompanied by three Arab Palestinian clergy, Jeries Salfity, Najib Cub'ain, and Fareed Oudeh, came to Beisan to formally bless and dedicate the hall as a temporary place for the worship of God until the Church of the Good Shepherd in Beisan would be built. Above the hall, my father built an apartment for his sister, Aunt Azeezeh.

There were many springs from the Gilboa mountains flowing into Beisan and irrigating its fertile land. Around the city were many citrus orchards—orange, grapefruit, cherimoya (*qashta*), and others. A few of the owners had become Anglicans and were good friends of our family. I have pleasant memories of visiting with my family and these friends in their orchards, especially on Sunday afternoons, playing with their children and having a wonderful time, while the adults were drinking coffee and some smoking cigarettes and the water pipe nargile.[3]

Most evenings, before going to bed, my father and mother would gather us around. We would sing hymns with father playing his diatonic accordion, play some games, say our family prayers, and then go to bed. We usually ended with one of three hymns after which we would say the

---

2. When we left Beisan in 1948, we were able to salvage the register of church services. I was surprised to discover the names of three dedicated laymen who alternated in taking the Sunday worship service, Habib Mansour, Ibrahim Oudeh, and Stifan Ateek. This register began after my father built the new hall. The first entry was October 1, 1934. The first page of the register reads in English and Arabic: Register of Services at Beisan, Palestine—Church of the Good Shepherd. Those who joined the church were known as Protestants.

3. In Arabic *huqqa* but in popular colloquial language, *argileh*. In the West, it is known as hookah or as hubble-bubble.

Lord's prayer. Many times, mother would try to rush so that she could relax after a hard day's work. But we always wanted to stay up to sing and dance. I have very fond memories of those evenings. Looking back, that family fellowship, the singing and playing, were an integral part of my own and my siblings' spiritual formation.

One day we had a severe hurricane in Beisan. The sound of the wind was frightening. A big tree behind our house was broken and shattered. I remember my father gathering us and reading Psalm 46, "God is our refuge and strength, a very present help in trouble," and then we prayed, asking God for protection and safety. Jesus Christ was at the center of our family life.

Often after school hours or whenever school was out, I was asked to stay in my father's shop to lessen my being a nuisance at home. One day I was stopped on my way home by three women who were on their way to my father's shop. They had a piece of metal and wanted to know whether it was gold. One of the women recognized me. She said, "Aren't you the son of the goldsmith?" I said, "I am." She said, "Take a look at this piece and tell me whether it is gold." I took the piece and looked at it as my father would have. Then I returned it to her and said, "This is not gold, it is copper." They continued to my father's shop and asked him. After proper examination through the help of acid, my father concluded that it was not gold. "This is what your son said. It's amazing, I knew it. The son of the goldsmith is a goldsmith," she replied. That evening my father asked me about this incident. This simple Bedouin woman believed that "the son of the goldsmith is born a goldsmith." Over the years, my father acquired a reputation of being trustworthy, honest, and having the fear of God. People came to like him and trust him.

Some Bedouin women used to come to my father's shop and ask him to write or make a charm for them. In the beginning he tried to explain to them that these charms had no power and they needed to trust God and pray to God for meeting their needs. If a bride did not become pregnant immediately after marriage, they wanted a charm or amulet to speed up the process. Some wanted charms to bring good luck or to avert evil. They would beg my father to make them. They would say, "We know that you are a person who fears God and we trust you. Please make a charm for us. God will answer your prayer." So, he started selecting a few verses from the Psalms, especially from Psalm 91, 27, or 34, and placing them in a silver case to give to them, telling them to trust God.

One time a Bedouin woman came with a bizarre request. She wanted a charm to be placed around the neck of her ewe so that she would give birth to a lamb. My father was not in the shop. My oldest brother Michel was. He tried his best to talk her out of what he considered a ridiculous and superstitious request, but she kept insisting. Out of frustration he asked her to return after half an hour and he would have it ready. He wrote a bunch of gibberish words that made no sense. He wrapped the paper and placed it in a little silver case and told the woman to place it around the ewe's neck and trust God for the outcome.

Several months later this woman came to the shop carrying a small lamb. Michel was not there. She gave it to my father and said, "my ewe was not having lambs. I asked your son to make her a charm and it worked. This is its firstborn and I want to give it to you as a gift." Later, when Michel came to the shop, he told my father his version of the story and the nonsensical things he had written on the charm. It was nice to have the lamb in our garden until the following Easter when it was slain for our Easter lunch.

Father practiced his Christian faith in his relationships with others. People who came to his shop knew well that there was no bargaining or haggling, and he never overpriced the items he made. When Michel finished elementary school, he started helping father in the shop. He observed the business ethics my father was practicing, but sometimes Michel would argue with my father regarding the art of bargaining. Michel was trying to convince father that bargaining was embedded in people's everyday business behavior when buying or selling, and he argued that it was wise to jack up the price a bit so that with haggling, you could bring it down to the right price. The buyers would feel good that they managed to bring down the price, and the sellers would reach the price they wanted. My father never accepted that logic and kept insisting that the honest and forthright way was to have a fixed price that was right and just and refuse any bargaining.

Once Michel used his bargaining skills in selling a piece of jewelry. He jacked up the price and after haggling he went down with the price and sold the item with a bigger profit margin. When father returned, Michel told him what happened and bragged about his shrewd business skills. My father was very angry and demanded that the extra profit be returned to the buyer. He also told Michel that he could not return home until the money was returned. Michel was out of the house for a few days, staying with friends until he found the buyer and gave back the money.

From one perspective, the story reflects my father's strict puritanical ethics, which he acquired from some of the missionaries, but on the other hand, it expresses the faith that cannot be separated from life and ethics. That is why my father was trusted and respected by the people of Beisan.

In those days, people did not know the value of old coins. After all, Beisan had plenty of layers of archeological sites. Infrequently, some of the Bedouins would bring father some coins they had found. If it was silver or gold, father would buy it and melt it. Many years later when I became aware of the value of ancient coins, I wondered how many coins my father could have saved had he known their real value.

One day, a woman came to the shop and showed my father a beautiful large coin. It was more like a medallion. After examining it, he realized that it was made of gold. My father bought it. After cleaning and polishing, it was revealed to be a Christian medallion. On one side, it had the nativity of Christ and on the other side was his baptism. He placed a ring on its side and made a beautiful gold chain and gave it to my mother as a gift. My mother wore it all the time, and now it is in the possession of our daughter Nevart.

My father loved working in his garden. Early in the morning and late in the afternoon he would spend time planting and tending it. Beisan was blessed with fertile soil and plenty of water. I have fond memories as a young boy helping my father care for the vegetables and fruit trees that he planted. A small canal of water used to go through our garden, flowing from one of the springs that originated from the Gilboa mountains. My father planted a variety of fruit trees including several types of delicious figs and pomegranates, and a large mulberry tree, which he planted in the middle of a courtyard surrounded by the three houses he had built behind our house. He also grew a number of banana and lemon trees in addition to the vegetable garden.

Another interesting memory had to do with the baking of bread. In those days most people prepared the dough for their Arab bread[4] at home but they had to take it to the closest public bakery to bake it. People had to wait in line for their turn. We called these places *el-foron*, which literally means "the oven." In those days, *el-foron* was the best place for the news of the town to circulate. Men, women, young and old, went to the *foron*. My older sisters took turns baking the bread, and because bread was our basic staple, and we were a large family, we consumed a large amount of it. Father and mother decided to build a special *foron* for our family on our land

---

4. Some refer to this bread as pocket bread or by its Greek name, pita.

that was fueled by kerosene. My sister Neda was the designated baker. This made it much easier and more convenient to bake our own bread at home.

Our life in Beisan was very comfortable and pleasant but it had its challenges. One day I was watching my father at work. Suddenly, the kerosene torch malfunctioned, and kerosene squirted on my father's clothes, and he was all ablaze. He jumped from the shop to the street, and I started screaming and many people from the other shops rushed out to extinguish the fire, using their jackets and whatever material they had. The fire was put out, but father suffered severe burns, especially to his hands and leg. I still remember that the skin on one of the hands had melted down. We managed to close the shop and to walk home. That night he had the chills; his whole body was shivering and shaking. Early the next day, a taxi took him to the Nazareth hospital. But for the grace and mercy of God we would have lost him. He spent several days in the hospital. Some of the scars he sustained remained visible on his body and especially on his hands for the rest of his life.

The Emerging Protestant Community

When the CMS decided to start a mission station in Beisan, my father welcomed it. In fact, it is very probable that father had a hand in inviting them. He was already known to them when he lived in Nablus and was anxious to expand their ministry. In order to help with their life and ministry in Beisan, father built a special house for the missionaries on our land, in addition to the two houses he had built, including the meeting hall. The special house consisted of three large rooms, a kitchen, and facilities. I am not aware whether the CMS contributed any money for the construction of this house, but I know that they lived rent free because they were doing the Lord's work.

God blessed the ministry in Beisan. At one point there were at least three British women missionaries. I remember Miss Nora Fisher, the sister of Geoffrey Fisher who later became the Archbishop of Canterbury (1945–61), Hannah Hurnard, and Miss Elisabeth Neatby.

The missionaries worked with children and women within the Christian community in Beisan, planting the love of God in the hearts and minds of people. As the small community of Protestants grew in number, the members began to raise funds for the building of the church. The construction began and my father was able to oversee the work. In 1941, the

Church of the Good Shepherd in Beisan was built from the black volcanic basalt local stones. It was dedicated by the Anglican Bishop in Jerusalem, George Francis Graham Brown (bishop from 1932–1942), on November 21, 1941, in the presence of ten Arab Palestinian Anglican clergy, the local Protestant community, a few British persons, and a good number of local Beisan residents. I was four years old, and I have a picture holding my sister Naomi's hand watching the procession of the bishop and clergy on their way to the new church.

Before the dedication service, my father and mother gave a big luncheon for the bishop, clergy, and the out-of-town guests. It took place on the large veranda in front of the new house my father had built for the missionaries. The whole celebration and dedication of the church was a wonderful, joyous event. My father was ecstatic. It was a dream come true. Although I was too young to remember, the picture with my sister Naomi remains a constant reminder of the occasion.

Muslims and Christians

In hindsight, the relationship between the various communities in Beisan was good. As a child, I never felt any discrimination or enmity between the Christian and Muslim communities. We lived as neighbors next to each other. I had a number of Muslim and Christian friends, but I was not aware of the importance of religious labels. I was never prevented from going into the home of a Muslim or Christian friend nor were they prevented from coming to our home. Maybe for adults, in those days, the religious labels were important, but only as stating a given fact, a reality of life rather than implicating feelings of bias or prejudice. We lived together as one Arab community of Christians and Muslims. It was superfluous even to use the word Palestinians because we were living in our homeland, Palestine. When a Muslim feast approached, I remember going with my friends to the mosque and climbing the steps of the minaret to announce the first day of the *'Eid*. I still recall the special words we chanted over and over again. Despite my young age, I was invited, more than once, to play our diatonic accordion at neighbors' (Muslim) weddings. I played a simple melody for people to dance to. I also know that my older brother Michel had several intimate friends, both Christians and Muslims. During his school days, Michel was chosen as the head of the Boy Scouts in Beisan although the number of Christians was small in the town.

In Nazareth, after our eviction from Beisan, I also had good friends who were Muslims and were fellow members of the Boy Scouts that belonged to our school. We were known as "Christ Evangelical Boy Scouts." The spirit of unity and togetherness was part of our life as a Palestinian community. The friendships and companionships we enjoyed together shunned prejudice and bigotry. I am thankful that the spirit of respect and equality within the community was instilled in my psyche as a child growing up in Beisan and Nazareth, and thankfully it stayed with me throughout my ministry and especially in the interfaith programs of Sabeel many years later.

Speaking the Truth

One hot summer day as I sat under the shade of one of the trees my father had planted, with my feet in the small canal of water that irrigated our garden, I noticed two boys around my age (nine or ten) fighting. One of the boys managed to free himself and started running, but the second boy pursued him while throwing stones at him. I noticed that in order to avoid one of the stones, the boy jumped from the sidewalk onto the main road when a big truck happened to be passing. The truck hit the boy and instantly killed him.

It did not take long before dozens of people with pitchforks and clubs gathered and wanted to kill the driver. The driver, terrified and panic-stricken, ran to our house, banging and pounding on the door. When my father opened the door, the driver pleaded with him for protection. Father invited him into the house and hid him. By then, the men outside reached our house and demanded that he turn the driver over to them so they could kill him. My father replied in the spirit of Arab culture and tradition, "A stranger has come into my house and asked for my protection. If you want to kill him, you have to kill me first." By then, a bigger crowd had gathered on our veranda, shouting and demanding to kill the man. A few minutes later, the British and Palestine police arrived at the scene, dispersed the crowd, and took the driver into custody. As the police were leaving our house, one officer asked, "Did anyone see what actually happened?" I replied, "I did," and the police wrote down my name.

A few weeks later I was asked to go to the courthouse in Beisan to give my testimony. My father took me to the courthouse, which was not far from his shop and told me to come to the shop when I was through. Before he left, father said to me, "Naim, just speak the truth. Tell the judge what you saw. Don't be afraid. God is with you."

I sat down outside the courtroom waiting my turn. Several men went in before me to witness; I was the last to be called. My young mind wondered about the testimony of those who went before me. I was sure that no one else had been on the street when the boy was killed. When I entered the room, I saluted the judge as my father told me. The judge looked me in the eye and said, "Tell me, son, what happened. What did you see?" I told the judge that the accident happened at noon and that there was no one around. The boy tried to avoid the stone by jumping into the street as the truck was passing and the accident happened. The judge thanked me, and I left the courthouse for my father's shop. When I returned home with my father for lunch, mother told me that the truck driver came by our house and kissed her hand saying, "Thank you, your son saved my life."[5]

This incident is imprinted in my memory, and I have passed it on to my children. The truth, simply told, has power. I will always remember my father telling me, "Naim, just speak the truth and don't be afraid. God is with you."

Siblings

I was blessed by a large family—seven sisters and two brothers. As an energetic and active boy, I often teased and pestered my sisters. Consequently, my father would spank me by hitting me with a stick on the bottom of my feet. My father believed that he was following the biblical injunction in disciplining me.[6] Later, with my own children, I used the stick, especially on the boys, as my father did, though more sparingly. When they grew up, I apologized to them for having done so. Now I watch them disciplining their children without the use of a stick and with better results and greater effect than the stick did for me.

I continue to get together with my brothers and sisters when possible. We spend time singing those wonderful hymns we first learned in Beisan and later in Nazareth. We have a number of accordions that my brother Saleem and I play, or we play the piano and organ. It is usually the most relaxing and therapeutic exercise we share. It rejuvenates and stimulates

5. Ateek, *Palestinian Christian Cry*, 35–36.

6. Prov 13:24, "Those who spare the rod hate their children, but those who love them are diligent to discipline them."

our spirits and souls. We have been doing this for many years and we will continue to do it as long as we can. It gives us great joy to be together, to reminisce, and to be thankful.

4

Growing Up in Nazareth[1]

WHEN THE ZIONIST MILITIAS dispossessed us and evicted us from Beisan, we were literally dumped on the outskirts of the town of Nazareth. Within a few hours, all the Beisan families who had land, property, homes, and businesses became refugees.

Nazareth was a town of ten thousand inhabitants, both Christians and Muslims, with the Christian community making up more than 50 percent of the population. Around the same time that we were evicted from Beisan, thousands of Palestinians—Christians and Muslims—from the surrounding villages were experiencing the same fate. Some were evicted by force like we were. Others fled in fright from their villages in lower Galilee, and most of them descended on Nazareth, while others fled to Lebanon. The Palestinians of the villages of Mijaidel, Ma'loul, Saffourieh, and Shajarah were all dispossessed and displaced. Many Palestinians of the city of Haifa fled in boats to Lebanon, while some came to Nazareth. The population of

---

1. "So, he [Joseph] got up, took the child and his mother and went to the land of Is-rael. But when he heard that Archelaus was reigning in Judea in place of his father Herod, he was afraid to go there. Having been warned in a dream, he withdrew to the district of Galilee" (Matt 2:21–22). Nazareth started as a small settlement town built by Aristobulus the Maccabean less than a century before Christ to Judaize the Galilee (Ateek, Duaybis, and Whitehead, *Bible and the Palestine-Israeli Conflict*, 32). Today, Nazareth has the larg-est Arab-Israeli population in Israel.

Nazareth swelled with Palestinian refugees. Most of them found shelter in schools, convents, or monasteries or lived with other families.

We arrived in Nazareth as refugees on May 26, 1948. For the first few weeks we stayed with our friend, Basmeh Khalaf, who had lived in our home in Beisan when she was giving sewing lessons to young women. Basmeh was visiting her relatives in Lebanon when we arrived in Nazareth, and we stayed in her house. My sister Hilda went with her husband and her two little girls, Lizzy and Samia, to the CMS orphanage while my family, fourteen of us including my brother Michel, his wife Adele, and their three-month-old daughter Wadad, stayed huddled together at Basmeh's two-bedroom house. Several days later, Miss Wyatt, the headmistress of the CMS orphanage (St. Margaret House) expressed her readiness to take my two youngest sisters, Naomi and Selma, as boarders. My father, who had been supporting the orphanage by sending them a year's supply of brooms, was very thankful for her kind gesture.

Although we were thankful to have a place to stay after our forced eviction, Basmeh's house was not adequate for our basic needs. It had no running water. My sisters had to fill up jars from Mary's Well during the night hours to avoid being seen during the day. It was too embarrassing for them. It was difficult to adjust in Nazareth, and we terribly missed our comfortable home in Beisan.

Several weeks later, the Rev. Khalil Jamal, the pastor of the Anglican church in Nazareth, invited my father to move with our whole family to stay at the Christ Church school building since the school year had closed early for the summer vacation because of the war. This move turned out to be a great relief for us. We had more space and a number of friends from our Episcopal church gave us mattresses, bedding, and blankets, as well as kitchen essentials. My parents had to sell some of the gold to buy some essential needs, especially clothing for us children.

A few months later, we were able to rent a house that was also owned by the Anglican Church. Our greater adjustment did not come until, several years later, we moved again to a bigger house, which we also rented from the church. In the meantime, my father and brother were able to rent a shop, buy tools, and resume their business as goldsmiths/jewelers. We were more fortunate than many other refugees because my father had been able to smuggle out the gold from Beisan.

On July 16, 1948, the Zionist Israeli forces occupied Nazareth. Again, there was no military resistance. We did not have an army to defend the town. I watched the Jewish soldiers entering the city on top of their military tanks. Some of them were wearing the Palestinian *kufieh*. In fact, some people of Nazareth thought, naively, that it was an Arab army that was coming to our defense. Some women started ululating for joy. But soon the ugly reality became clear.

Eventually, the Israeli army was able to conquer the whole of Galilee. Israel did not stop with what the Partition Plan had allotted to it. Most of Galilee, including Nazareth, was not supposed to be part of the state of Israel, but the Zionists had their own political agenda, and they had the military power to implement it.

Military Law

The government of Israel imposed military law on all the Palestinians who remained in what became the state of Israel. No one in Galilee was able to leave his/her place of residence without a military permit. We were confined to our own living areas. People had to stand for hours in line to get a military permit to leave Nazareth, and many were denied. Most Jewish areas were out of bounds. People who violated the law were jailed and/or fined.

One day a friend and I wanted to visit another friend in the Rambam Hospital in Haifa. We took the bus from Nazareth to Haifa, and, on the way, we were stopped at a checkpoint and the police came on board to check our permits. I had a permit, but my friend did not, and he was arrested. Since I was now on my own, I left the bus and returned to Nazareth to bail him out.

Military law was imposed for eighteen years (1948–1966) on the Palestinian population. The word Palestinian became taboo. We were known as "the non-Jewish minorities of Israel": Christians, Muslims, Druze, etc. The more generic word "Arab" replaced the more specific name "Palestinian." When we returned to school, we discovered that the word "Palestine" had disappeared from history and geography books in the new Israeli curriculum. It was a clever attempt to erase our Palestinian identity.[2] Our Palestinian flag was banned,[3] and it seemed clear that our exile was going to be permanent.

2. The first IDs issued by Israel after 1948 included the word "Palestinian." Later this was omitted. But, for us, our identity was never in question. In spite of Israel's effort to erase the Palestinian identity, it was deeply ingrained in us. It was who we were.

3. It was many years later before I even learned the colors of the Palestinian flag (black, red, green, and white).

Humanitarian Aid

The United Nations and church organizations from abroad started sending humanitarian aid to the Palestinian refugees. My father offered his services and became connected with the Sisters of Nazareth Convent in the distribution of food, clothing, and goods to the Palestinian refugees in Nazareth and the vicinity.

For many international donors, it seemed easier to give to charity than to work for justice. Israel flouted the UN resolutions that called for the return of refugees and the implementation of international law.

In spite of the tragedy of Palestine and the pain and agony of many family members separated by the war, people had to accept the reality of their new life under the occupation of Israel and the loss of Palestine. Indeed, we missed Beisan and the comfort of our home, but we had no choice but to accept the new reality that had been forced on us. I used to hear my father and mother say, "May God's will be done." I believe this level of trust in God helped us survive the tragedy. I remember my father's words, "All things would work together for good for those who loved the Lord" (Rom 8:28).

As to our family, we were thankful to God that we remained together. We did not lose faith and kept our trust in God's goodness and mercy. It took some time, but slowly we were able to adjust to our new reality of life. My sister Hilda and her family moved to West Jerusalem where Issa, her husband, found a job at the French Consulate due to his multilingual skills. My sister Huda started teaching elementary school at our Anglican Christ Church School in the center of old town Nazareth. My sister Neda was employed by the CMS orphanage as housekeeper and later became a second-grade teacher at the same school. My sister Fida found a job with the Southern Baptist American missionaries that had started a home for orphans and poor Palestinian children. My sister Naomi continued her studies at the orphanage and completed her second year of high school and then started teaching school. Selma and I were registered at Christ Church elementary school. Saleem stayed at home because he was too young to go to school.

As already mentioned, my father and brother Michel started their business again. Before the Palestinian Nakba, Nazareth had one goldsmith shop. With the influx of refugees into Nazareth, no less than five new goldsmith/jewelers' shops opened up.

The Brazil Plan

In the early 1950s, our church remnant in Israel faced a serious threat that jeopardized its very existence.

In 1951, Assis Rafiq Farah, the Anglican minister in Haifa, discovered a conspiracy instigated by Israeli government officials in collusion with a prominent layman of our church who was at the time the head of our depleted and weakened Majma (church council). The government of Israel was ready to transfer the remnant Episcopal church community in Israel to Brazil. They would be given land and would be settled comfortably there. In lieu of that, Israel would take all the Episcopal churches' property, including the church buildings as well as the property of the individual members. This plan was presented as if the government of Israel was concerned about the well-being of the Christian community and was doing it a favor.

In January 1951, the church council was called into session in Haifa to vote on the Brazil plan. Most of the delegates condemned the scandalous plan. They deposed the chairman for his collusion with the Israeli officials and replaced him with Rev. Farah. Those faithful church members considered the plan as treachery, and with great courage and heightened emotions the scheme was exposed and vetoed down.

Had the scandal not been averted, it would have been a black and shameful blot and disgrace to our church. Thank God, it was prevented by the courage, integrity, and unity of those few members who rose up under the leadership of Rev. Farah. They took a stand to protect the church they loved. Indeed, they were the simple folks; many of them were themselves refugees who had been uprooted by Israel, having lost their homes and towns.

I still remember to this day my father coming home and telling us what happened in the church council meeting. I was a teenager at the time and was not fully aware of the negative impact of that story. I thank God that my father was one of those who had the courage to stand for what was right, honorable, and just. Thus, our church remained in its homeland to witness to the love and justice of God despite the tragedy of the Nakba.

The Village of Reineh

Although my father and mother had a huge responsibility looking after the needs of the family, my father could not stay away from assisting in the local Anglican Church as he used to be active in the Church of the Good

Shepherd in Beisan. He offered his services to Assis Khalil Jamal, the minister of both Nazareth and Reineh churches. Assis Khalil asked my father to help him in conducting the Sunday morning prayer services in the village of Reineh, less than two miles north of Nazareth.

In those days, Nazareth had very few taxi cabs and a few private cars. Every Sunday, my father would walk the two miles to the church in Reineh, where he would lead the service of morning prayer, preach, and then return to Nazareth on foot. Almost every Sunday I would accompany my father. I got to know the people in the church well and it gave me a chance to hear my father's sermon. Oftentimes, while walking to the village, I would share with my father my dream of becoming an Assis and serving Christ in our church.

Eventually, we were able to buy a small used pump organ that I was able to fix. Since we had lost our small accordion in Beisan, the little organ gave a new life and joy to our family. Music and the singing of hymns were always an important part of our family life.

In anticipation of becoming a minister, I started taking piano lessons at St. Joseph girls' school in Nazareth from a Catholic Irish sister. She was Sister Archangela, but she was simply known as "Sister." I went to the girls' school every day to practice, since we did not have a piano at home. Because I was highly motivated, my music skills and my playing improved quickly. Before too long, I was playing the small harmonium in the Reineh church. Sister continued to give me piano lessons for several years until one day she suggested that I look for a more professional teacher. For a few years, I went to Haifa every week to take piano lessons from a Jewish teacher.

Many years later after I was ordained, I looked up Sister. She had left Nazareth and was retired at St. Joseph Convent in Jerusalem. She recognized me and I thanked her profusely for her role in preparing me for ministry through her patient piano teaching. My pastoral ministry was blessed by the gift of music, which Sister nourished and developed in me.

The Baptist High School

After completing the Anglican Christ Church primary school, I moved to the American School in Nazareth. This is the way people referred to it. It was run by Southern Baptist missionaries. Later it became known as the Baptist school. For multiple years, the Americans provided the music for the school and church. As my piano playing improved, I started playing for the school's daily chapel assembly. Later I was asked to play the organ for the Baptist Church Sunday services.

On Sunday afternoons, I used to accompany some of the American missionaries and the local Baptist pastors to some of the villages where they held Sunday school for the children. By then, my family was able to purchase a diatonic accordion like the one we had in Beisan. I would take it with me to lead the singing, and the children enjoyed it. One of the villages I enjoyed visiting was Turan. Many Sunday afternoons, when we reached the village, the American missionary would open the back door of the station wagon where I would sit dangling my feet so that I could play my accordion. He would drive through the village, and the children would follow us to attend the Sunday school.

Graduation

In 1956, I graduated from high school. Although I was one of a few students in my class who graduated with over 90 percent grade-point average for the four years of high school, I could not march in the graduation procession because I was playing the piano for my graduating class.

At the beginning of my senior year in high school, I sent a letter to the Episcopal church council (Majma) expressing my desire to study for the ministry. I was informed that they would be in touch. When I did not hear from them by the end of the school year, I accepted a job as secretary of the American school. This was a new position that the American principal, Herman Petty, was creating. In fact, he invited me to take the job. It was a good job, and I was very pleased and thankful to have it. I thought that it could help me save some money when I went abroad to study without burdening my father with my expenses.

At the school I was always busy. I assisted the principal in any task he assigned me. I had to collect school fees, prepare teachers' salaries, type students' exams in three languages, Arabic, English, and Hebrew, and do substitute teaching whenever one of the teachers was absent. In those days, very few people played the piano, so I continued to play the piano for the daily chapel services as I had done during most of my high school years. In addition, I had to lead the chapel service once a week by giving a meditation.

The first school year went by quickly. It ended without hearing a word from the Majma. When I checked, no decision had been made. It was not as if we had an excess of clergy. In fact, we had a great shortage of clergy. The

Majma in Israel was passing through very difficult times since the Nakba. Our people were under military law. There was no freedom of movement. The Majma lacked resources, and it was difficult to make decisions. The church in Israel was totally separated from our church on the West Bank, including East Jerusalem and Jordan, where most of our Palestinian members and clergy were living. It is, therefore, important to pause and clarify the political-historical changes that led to the shortage of clergy for our Anglican/Episcopal church.

Church in Crisis

The last meeting of the Majma before the Nakba was held at the YMCA in Nazareth from April 27 to May 2, 1947. Despite the increasing political tensions in the country, thirteen clergy and twenty-two laymen attended. They came from all over Palestine as well as Jordan. This took place one year before we were dispossessed from Beisan. My father attended the Majma representing the Church of the Good Shepherd.

At that time, we did not have an indigenous bishop. The head of the Majma was an elected senior minister. The English bishop came only to officiate at confirmations. The election of an indigenous Arab bishop was a hope that was not yet realized. It was courageous for the Majma to have its annual meeting in Nazareth, and the choice of Nazareth as a venue was also important because the leaders of our church had been avoiding the big cities where the Zionist militias were active in violence and terror.

Our three largest Episcopal churches in Palestine were in Haifa, Jaffa, and Jerusalem. St. John the Evangelist in Haifa was the largest, with over 1,200 members. St. Paul's Church in West Jerusalem and St. Peter's in Jaffa had approximately 450 members each. Many of the members were successful businessmen, lawyers, doctors, and engineers. Some had been forced out while others left with their families to escape the violence and terror of the war. Many of those who left Haifa and Jaffa went to Beirut, Lebanon, by sea and established a vibrant church there. Out of the 1,200 church members in Haifa only 150 were left. Of the 450 members in Jaffa only two families remained. Our historic St. Paul's Church in West Jerusalem was abandoned. A handful of Christian families stayed and continued to live in West Jerusalem under Israeli rule; others moved to East Jerusalem. Most of our members, however, went to Amman, Jordan, and established the Church of the Redeemer, which became the largest in the diocese. As already mentioned, churches that lost the most members were those in the three major cities of Palestine.

Within a few weeks after the Nakba, most of our clergy had left Palestine with their families. We were left with two ministers to look after ten small and largely depleted congregations. The only congregation that increased in number was Nazareth due to the influx of refugees from the surrounding towns. What helped those ministers was the presence of lay readers who conducted morning or evening prayer services in some of the churches while the two ministers went once a month to administer Holy Communion. My father was one of three lay readers who helped in conducting the worship services and looking after the pastoral needs of the remnant communities.

My Call to Ministry Is Energized

This was the picture of our church in Israel after the Nakba. This was the historical and political background that led to the weakening number of our church congregations, and the absence of clergy that consequently created the shortage of ministers and pastors.

I was aware that our church was in dire need of ministers, and it was difficult for our small and debilitated Majma to find the financial resources and to make the organizational arrangements for my study abroad. Nevertheless, it was difficult to watch the months go by while waiting for the decision to be made.

As I was living in great anticipation of going out to study, my frustration was heightening. I was reminded that just before my graduation from high school, Rev. Paul Rowden, one of the Baptist missionaries, a very spiritual and godly man, invited me to his office in the school and asked me whether I still felt a call to the ministry. I answered affirmatively. He made it clear to me that if I joined the Baptist Church, the Baptist mission board would be ready to send me to college and seminary and then I could return home to Nazareth and serve the Lord in Galilee. I thanked him for his kindness and generous offer, but I made it clear that since I was a little boy in Beisan, I felt God's call to the ministry of my church. This call never wavered. I explained to him what happened to our church during the Nakba and how most of the clergy were dispossessed, and that there was a great need for new ministers to serve the various congregations that were left in Israel.

Rev. Rowden was very gracious and listened to what I said. We spent more time discussing the importance and need of ministry, and at the end he asked to say a prayer for me. After the prayer, I thanked him again and left. In some way, this meeting energized the call in me, and I decided to continue to wait for God's time. I remembered my father's frequent saying, "May God's will be done." Deep in my heart I knew that God would guide my future. I only needed to continue to trust and wait on the Lord.

Jubilee Jamboree

The year 1957 marked the 50th anniversary of the inception of the Boy Scouts movement, and the 100th anniversary of the birth of its founder, Robert Baden-Powell. Approximately thirty thousand scouts from around the world were going to celebrate the Jubilee Jamboree in Sutton Coldfield, England, in August 1957. Four Israeli Arab scouts, a Muslim, a Druze, a Catholic, and I, were chosen to represent the Arab scouts in Israel together with a small contingent of Jewish scouts. We sailed from the port of Haifa, stopping in Italy, France, England, and Scotland. We traveled together for almost a month, sometimes staying in youth hostels, other times with Jewish families along the way.

This was my first trip abroad and it was a very good experience for me. It helped me develop good relationships and friendships with the Jewish Boy Scouts as well as my fellow Arabs. It also helped me practice both the English and Hebrew languages.

One negative incident happened at the start of the trip. In those days it was very difficult to take any hard currency abroad. Mr. Herman Petty, the American school principal, wanted to give me a check for one hundred dollars so that I could have some pocket money. He arrived late to the Haifa seaport to say goodbye, but I was already on the ship. He tried to pass the check to me by slipping it inside the case of a hatchet that I had forgotten. The police were watching, and they caught the check before I received it. They debated whether to take me to jail, but finally decided to let me continue the trip with the Boy Scouts.

The ship sailed but I kept anxiously wondering what had happened to Mr. Petty or to my family. Did the police take any of them to jail? Did this episode jeopardize the legal presence of the American missionary? There was no way to find out! There were no cell phones in those days, so I had to endure the agony throughout the journey.

The sea journey ended in Italy. From there we traveled by bus the rest of the way. We met with many Jewish groups during our travels, and in some places, we sang and danced to Hebrew folk music. Looking back on those days, we were like a showcase. We presented a positive image of Israel where Jews, Muslims, Druze, and Christians were "peacefully" living together. At that time, Israel was living its heyday when secular Zionism and the Labor party ruled almost supreme, with no right-wing rivals that were worth mentioning.

In some places, we stayed in student hostels, other times in camps where Jews were placed awaiting their Aliyah.[4] When we got to England and Scotland, we stayed as guests in Jewish homes. I was always thankful for the gracious hospitality and kindness of the families I was assigned to. I always made it clear that I was an Israeli Arab[5] and if asked about my background I told my story about Beisan and how we came to Nazareth as refugees.

The experience at the Jamboree was very memorable. The campground in Sutton Coldfield was huge. Every country was assigned an area for its scout troop. We pitched our tents, decorated our space and set up our exhibit. There were various activities every day throughout the twelve days of the festivities. Thousands of people from the outside came to visit. Since my English language skills were good, I had many opportunities to make friends and enjoy the experiences during our time there.

After we returned home, I was summoned by the head of police at Haifa's seaport from where we had sailed. He seemed kind and asked me how my trip to the Boy Scout Jamboree was. Then he took out from the drawer the hundred-dollar check which the police had confiscated and asked me to endorse it on the back. This caught me by surprise, and I hesitated for a moment. I then kindly declined and basically told him that I could not do it. I also said that it would be nice if he would give it to me so that I could return it to the American school principal. This seemingly kind officer turned ugly, and he started threatening me and pressuring me to sign the check, saying that if I did not, he would take me to court, and I would end up in prison. I was shaken by his threats, but I kept insisting that I could not do it because the check was not his, and it was not right for him to take the money. If he wanted to take me to court so be it, but I would not

4. Their "ascent" to Israel.

5. The word "Palestinian" returned to use after the 1967 war and the occupation of East Jerusalem, the West Bank, and the Gaza Strip.

sign the check. Eventually he asked me to leave and threatened to see me in court. I never heard from him again.

I thanked God for giving me the strength and courage to stand for what was morally right.

The trip to Europe and to the Jubilee Jamboree was a wonderful and amazing experience. I saw the beauty and wonder of many sites. I was introduced to the rich history of Europe through visits to the cathedrals, museums, and castles as well as meeting and interacting with people from all walks of life. In retrospect, it was a maturing experience and an amazing introduction for me before going abroad to study. It broadened and enriched my outlook on life.

There was, however, another side to this experience. Our life in Nazareth under the occupation and military law insulated us. Thankfully, my family had a very close-knit relationship with one another. Our love for one another and our love of Christ strongly bonded us. We never experienced feelings of loneliness. Our lines of communication were always open between and among us. Then the opportunity presented itself to take part in the Jamboree away from home for several weeks. When the initial euphoria and excitement of traveling abroad passed, I started to feel homesick. There was no way to get in touch. I sent home postcards regularly and expressed to my family the joy of visiting the various lovely places in Europe, but at the same time, this deep homesickness, which I couldn't explain or understand, was very painful. At times, I could hardly wait to get back home. I was counting the days and the hours to return.

When I arrived home and saw my family again, it was as if a heavy psychological load had been taken off me. The homesickness immediately vanished, and I basked in the joy of being back home and sharing with my family and friends my amazing experiences of the trip.

Yet only a few days later, I started wishing I could go back abroad. I still remember how I was introspectively engaged within myself, trying to understand those deep emotions that gripped me when I was away from home. This experience turned out to be very valuable, especially during my first year of study in the United States. Whenever I felt a deep homesickness, I came back to this trip. It became a therapeutic device that used to reinvigorate and restore me to normal healthy feelings and away from the pain of separation and homesickness. Whenever I had those deep feelings of homesickness, I would go out for a walk or go to the gym. It helped me to snap out of it.

Another source of help was to remember God's call and my ultimate objective of serving Christ that I always desired. It helped me to count God's blessings, and my gratitude to God for providing me with the education I needed to reach my objective. Later, these two therapeutic reminders, especially the second, kept me sane and safe during my seven years of study abroad.

Going Back to Beisan

On May 15, 1958, ten years after the Palestinian Nakba, the Israeli military governor allowed all Israeli Arabs to move freely and without a military permit to visit anywhere they wanted to go in Israel. The occasion marked the tenth anniversary of Israel's Independence Day. My family took advantage of this day. We rented a truck with seats like a bus and went down to Beisan—father and mother and all the family. My father was now sixty-six years old. Michel had married Wadi'a Khouriyeh after the death of his wife Adele. My sister Naomi was married to Emil Bashlawi. Saleem, who was three years old when we left Beisan, was now thirteen, and I, who was eleven years old when we were evicted, was now twenty-one. We went with mixed emotions. What had become of our home? Had they demolished it, or were people living in it? What about my father's shop? Were they taking care of our garden? Were they enjoying the pomegranates, the bananas, and the figs? We were going back to our beloved Beisan with our individual and collective memories, but we were going with great anxiety, nervousness, and trepidation.

When we arrived in Beisan, our house that was on the main street was still there intact. My father went down and knocked on the door, and a woman answered. Father explained that we used to live there, and asked if we could just take a look? The woman very rudely said, "This is our home, and you are not welcome. Go away." She shut the door in our face. We went around and looked at the other houses that my father had built. It was clear that Jews had divided our property into smaller units and several families were living there.

We drove through Beisan and looked around. The Orthodox Church across the street was still standing, but there were no doors and people were using it as an outhouse. The Roman Catholic Church was used as the headquarters of a Jewish political party. The belfry on top of our small Anglican church was broken and the building was used as a shop. The mosque was still standing but the minaret was demolished and all the area around it was destroyed. To the east of the town, the Muslim and Christian cemeteries were totally neglected, and a new Jewish cemetery was founded. (My grandfather was buried in the Christian cemetery in Beisan.) Close to the girls' school was a barber shop where I used to have my hair cut; it was still used as a barber shop but with a Jewish barber. Most of the market and industrial areas of town, where father's shop had been, were demolished. It was a very painful and agonizing experience, a source of anguish and distress for all of us, especially for my father and mother.

We returned to Nazareth with great sadness and broken hearts, not realizing the heavy impact this visit had on my parents. Everywhere I looked, I had memories of friends and childhood experiences of a wonderful past in Beisan. It was like living a dream again that had turned into a nightmare. It was as if I were two people. Within me was the child who loved Beisan, my beautiful childhood, our family life, our singing, dancing, and praying together. The sound of our diatonic accordion. It was in Beisan, as a child, where I came to love Jesus through the example of my father and mother. There was, however, another person within me, now twenty-one years of age looking at the tragedy of the Nakba and asking many penetrating questions. Why were we thrown out at gunpoint? What wrongs had we done to forfeit our home, our wonderful town, and our country? What crimes did we commit that warranted our dispossession and disinheritance? Surely, it was not through any fault of our own. It was not until years later that I came to understand that this was the result of the political intrigue and lust of Zionism. It was due to Western religious beliefs that were based on faulty biblical and theological interpretations. We were pawns in the hands of colonial and imperial power politics that were manipulated by a Zionist ideology that coveted the land of Palestine and conspired to displace and eliminate its indigenous people. Indeed, the Palestinians paid the price for the Western Christian guilt of antisemitism against the Jewish people. The Palestinians were especially betrayed by British and American political leaders who were themselves victims of a Christian heresy concocted by Protestant biblicism that placed prophecy above God's justice, truth, love, and mercy.

Our fateful visit to Beisan with my parents was another living reminder of the reality of injustice and oppression in the world, expressed particularly in the experience of our Palestinian people. It provided an opportunity to renew my commitment to serve Christ in his church and even outside the church by working for justice, truth, peace, and reconciliation wherever God would lead me. It was a renewal of my response to God's call that never wavered within me.

The mental, psychological, emotional, and physical impact of this visit on my father was immense. It was more than any of us could have imagined. A few weeks after we returned to Nazareth, my father had a stroke and never recovered from it. The stroke affected his speech and legs. He was not able to speak plainly nor was he able to walk properly. My mother had to nurse him until his death on September 2, 1960.

A Time to Decide

Before the second school year was approaching its completion, the Rev. Ronald Adeney came to see me in Nazareth. Ronald was an Anglican minister working in Israel for a British society called the "Church's Ministry among Jewish People" (CMJ). Although he had a deep commitment for the conversion of the Jewish people, he had become aware of the Palestinian Nakba and understood the predicament of the Palestinian people and their need for justice and the establishment of their own state alongside the state of Israel.

Ronald started by asking me about my job at the Baptist school and then slowly the conversation moved to talking about my future. He explained to me about the difficulties the Anglican bishop in Jerusalem and the Majma were having in finding the right place for me to study. He mentioned that most of our clergy in the past were trained at the Near East School of Theology (NEST) in Beirut, Lebanon. But since I was an Israeli citizen, I was not allowed to leave Israel to any of the neighboring states, since none of the Arab states recognized the legitimacy of Israel. England was a second option, but the Majma was afraid that once I went to England, I might decide to stay there and not come back. India could be the best possibility, but the Majma had not been able to arrange it so far; hence, I needed to wait. It was clear that Rev. Adeney had been sent to deliver this message to me. It was now up to me to decide the best line of action.

After consulting with my parents and family and much prayer, I wrote a letter to the Majma requesting to withdraw my application to study for the ministry. I also said that I still felt that God was calling me to the ministry of the church, and I trusted that God would guide me into the future and would open the way for my education and seminary training.

Leaving for the States

Subsequently, I went to my boss, Mr. Herman Petty, the principal of the American school, and asked him if he could help me find a scholarship in a college in the States so that I could continue my education. Within a few weeks, he was able to find me a full scholarship at Hardin-Simmons University in Abilene, Texas.[6]

I completed my third year as school secretary in Nazareth and, in July 1959, I said goodbye to my family in Nazareth and left for the States. The hardest thing for me was to leave my father, whose health was gradually deteriorating. When I kissed him goodbye, I was not sure whether I would see him again. Although he was not in a position to leave the house due to his condition, my mother wisely decided to bring him to the Lydda airport (later Ben Gurion) so that he could see me get on the plane and fly out of the country. In those days, people could watch the passengers as they walked to the plane and wave their goodbyes. A number of our family accompanied me to the airport to bid me farewell.

My father, periodically, would ask about me and show his frustration at my absence, and my mother would explain to him that I had gone to America to study to become Assis. She would even show him my picture at the entrance of the plane waving goodbye, and that would calm him down.

6. The university was founded as Abilene Baptist College in 1891 by the Sweetwater Baptist Association and a group of cattlemen and pastors who sought to bring Christian higher education to the Southwest. The university has been associated with the Baptist General Convention of Texas since 1941.

Part II

Formation

5

Hardin-Simmons University (H-SU)

I FLEW TWA TO New York, then changed planes to Dallas and boarded another small plane to Abilene, Texas. My arrival in the summer of 1959 transported me into another historic period, this one being the time of desegregation in the southern US following the Brown v. Board of Education ruling by the US Supreme Court in 1954. Hardin-Simmons University was affected like all educational institutions, and I was a close-up observer as the university integrated black students into its common life in 1962. My own education seeing the US trying to escape its racist system had begun before I attended my first class.

When I arrived, I was met by a middle-aged woman who took me through the Hardin-Simmons University campus to the house of Mrs. Hearn, an elderly woman who lived on the edge of the campus. Since it was still the summer vacation and the dorms were closed, it was arranged for me to rent a room in Mrs. Hearn's house until the end of the summer.

The landscape of Abilene in West Texas was different from anything I'd seen before. The whole area was flat with no hills around. In the summer it was hot and there was no air conditioning in those days. A few people had air-coolers but that was no match to the efficiency of air conditioning.

My first impression of the people I met was pleasant. I found them very warm and friendly. From the first week of my arrival, I was able to find work on campus. I joined a crew who were busy doing maintenance work preparing the university for the fall semester. I moved furniture, painted classrooms, used sheetrock to complete an apartment building, many things I had not done before. I had to acquire a new vocabulary about names of tools and building material. It was an important experience that I needed. Most of all, it was important to meet people and work with them. Slowly, I became acquainted and acclimated to the campus, to its buildings and the various departments. I was thankful that my fellow workers were patient in teaching and guiding me. They asked me where I had come from, and when I answered "Nazareth" they were often confused, since there was also a Nazareth in Texas. My answer always opened up more discussion as I shared what life was like back home and started conversations that helped me get to know people and make friends.

It soon became clear that the English that I had learned at school was different from the English these Texans were speaking. Indeed, I had an accent, but some of them seemed to have a worse accent than mine, and it was difficult to understand each other. The Texas drawl seemed, at times, a foreign language to me. In fact, it was embarrassing to keep saying, "Excuse me, say that again."

The food was also different. There was a drug store close to the campus where I used to go and eat. It was there that I had my first hamburger. I liked it and whenever I did not know what else to eat, I would always order a hamburger. At times I ate hamburgers for breakfast, lunch, and supper. Obviously, things changed when the semester started, and I was exposed to the variety of the American menu in the cafeteria.

At Hardin-Simmons there were a few foreign students from Europe and Asia but no one from the Middle East. It was not easy to find even olive oil. I often longed for Arab food, but it was not available, nor were its ingredients.

Every Sunday I wrote a letter to my parents, and they received it two weeks later. My sister Neda used to write to me regularly on their behalf. She always ended her letters with the words, "Keep on the Rock." It was a source of strength to me, a constant reminder to keep my faith strong in Christ. Many years later, I searched the internet and found the story that my sister Neda was quoting that sentence from: *Saved at Sea: A Lighthouse Story* by Mrs. O. F. Walton, 1887. The grandfather in the story kept telling his grandson, "Be sure you keep on the rock."[1] This sentence has accompanied me for many years of my life, and the song that is based on it has

---

1. Walton, *Saved at Sea*.

always inspired and strengthened me, "On Christ the solid rock I stand, all other ground is sinking sand."[2]

Since I was sure that I would be going to seminary, I chose not to major in religious studies but in chemistry, yet took religious studies as a minor. One of the main reasons for taking a science major was that I was not a fast reader in English, and I was afraid that I would not be able to cope with all the reading assignments.

Years later, I felt that a major in history, sociology, or psychology would have been more helpful to me in ministry than chemistry. However, there were no regrets, because science gave me useful training in the discipline of the scientific method of thinking. I became active in the Science Club on campus and later became its president.

Academically, the first year was the hardest because of the new system of education and the need for greater English fluency. Once I was able to overcome those challenges, I did well, and thankfully I was able to make the dean's list for two consecutive years.

The four years at Hardin-Simmons were rewarding in many ways. They provided me with many varied experiences both on as well as off campus. I was thankful to God for coming to H-SU. It had fewer than two thousand students at that time and it was easy to meet new people and make friends. I always felt accepted, included, and welcomed by others. During my time there, I had a German, a Hungarian Jew, and a Texan as roommates. Helmut Rueb came from Germany because he had an American girlfriend. I believe that after completing his studies, they were married. Charles Fodor left Hungary when the Soviets occupied it in 1956. We had many good and stimulating discussions about our backgrounds. Once I asked him why he did not immigrate to Israel? His answer surprised me. He said, "There are too many Jews there." After graduation from H-SU, he married an American woman and decided to stay in the States. Don Wadkins was my American roommate. We had four other friends living next to us and we spent good times together. I lost track of Don after he left the university. Many years later, we found each other again and renewed our friendship. He became an active member of Sabeel and visited Jerusalem more than once. I was blessed with every one of my roommates, and I pray that wherever their journey has taken them, they are well.

2. Mote, "On Christ."

A Providential Meeting

In the fall of 1959, one of the first people I met outside the university campus was Joseph Housson. I believe it was providential. One day during my first year, a young man in his early thirties came to the university asking whether there was an Arab student studying there. It did not take a long time to find me, since I was the only Arab student around. Joe seemed to be a kind and friendly gentleman and it was easy to connect. He was working for Mobile Oil and was living in Eastland, a small town approximately sixty miles east of Abilene.

He told me his story. His father immigrated to the United States from Syria and lived in East Texas where he married Bess Shirley, an American woman from that area, and they had three children. His father never returned to Syria and continued his comfortable life in Texas until he was killed in a car accident just a few years before we met. Joe added that when he was going through his father's papers, he found a bunch of letters written in Arabic and that was why he came to Hardin-Simmons, hoping to find an Arab student who could translate those letters.

Our meeting was the beginning of a life-long relationship and friendship. The letters his father received from his family in Syria were about social and family matters, the kind a father writes to his son to check on his health and his life in America. Joe started coming to visit me at school and oftentimes we would go out to eat. On some weekends, he would pick me up and take me to Eastland. He had a room at the Alhambra hotel and would always rent another room for me. On Sunday night he would bring me back to the dorm.

Joe and I enjoyed many stimulating discussions on religion, politics, Middle East history, and other varied subjects. He was always anxious to know about our family life and culture back home. Joseph Housson was God-sent. He became an older brother to me, and it was always good to see him and spend time with him. It was especially important on those weekends when most students went back home, and he provided a home for me that lessened any feelings of homesickness. I would tell my family about Joe and his kindness and friendship in my weekly letters to Nazareth and asked them if one of my sisters could write and thank him on behalf of my parents. Later, I was very happy when I found out that my sister Neda had written Joe and expressed to him my family's gratitude for being so kind and generous toward me.

As summer was approaching, Joe asked me whether I would like to spend the summer at Eastland. He was hoping that I could find a job there. I did a few small jobs that demanded physical labor, and also got my driver's license. Later, Joe helped me find a job near Clyde, Texas, where the United States was building missile sites around Abilene. I had a physically strenuous job working for a construction company. I was feeding the concrete mixer with cement and sand most of the day. At times, I had to work over twelve hours a day and I would return to my room in Clyde exhausted, with thick dirt covering my face and hair. In spite of the hard and demanding labor, it was a good job and it paid well, enough to give me pocket money for the next school year.

My Father's Death

At the end of the summer and just before I returned to the university for my second year, I received a telegram from my brother Michel that read: "Your father died on September 2, 1960. His suffering and pain are over. He is now with the Lord." I was overwhelmed with deep sadness and grief on the one hand, and on the other hand, I felt a sense of relief, comfort, and thanksgiving. I sat in my room for a long time reflecting on my father and what he meant to me. I reflected on our life in Beisan, which was the epitome of my childhood experiences. I gave thanks to God for my father's life, for his strong faith and trust in God, as well as his love and service to Christ. I also thanked God for my mother and prayed that God would give her comfort and strength so that she could enjoy good health after the long months of dedicated care of my father during his illness. I entrusted my father to the love and mercy of Christ. I also prayed for my loved ones in Nazareth so that Christ would embrace them with his care and love.

A few weeks later, I received a letter from my mother. She had found a piece of paper in my father's Bible written in his handwriting and addressed, "To my son Naim. Read Psalm 37:5." I rushed to my Arabic and then my English Bible and read, "Commit thy way unto the Lord, trust also in him, and he shall bring it to pass." This was my father's bequest to me: to commit, to trust, and to let God act. One of the most frequently uttered words by my father was: May God's will be done. In this beautiful verse from the Psalms, I felt that my father was blessing me and urging me, charging me, and assuring me of God's active involvement in my life and future ministry.

A few days later, I returned to the university for my second year of schooling. I was not aware that Neda's letter to Joe expressing my family's gratitude for his friendship and kindness to me had initiated a regular correspondence between the two that lasted for over one year.

One day Joe told me that he would like to marry my sister Neda. This came as a big surprise to me. He told me that although he had multiple woman friends, he did not feel that any of them was the right person for him. I immediately made it clear to Joe about the obstacles that I could foresee. I mentioned that although Joe's father had come from Syria and he was fully Arab, Joe was born and brought up in Texas as a fully American man, and very much a product of American culture. It would not be easy for him to marry a woman without dating her and getting to know her well. Furthermore, and this was the most important point, in my Palestinian culture, we don't have divorce. Once we get married it is "until death do us part." These were important considerations that needed to be taken into account. We spent a long time discussing this. Finally, we agreed to ask Neda to come for a summer visit and if things didn't work out, she would return to Nazareth and resume her teaching job at the orphanage.

As best as I could, I made several arrangements for Neda. I arranged for her to stay with Mrs. Hearn, in the room I stayed in when I first came to the States. We also agreed that Joe and Neda would then have a chance to get to know each other before they made any decision.

Joe paid for her plane ticket to the States, and on March 24, 1962, Neda arrived at Love Field Airport in Dallas. In those days, she was permitted to take out with her $150 only. I was there to meet her with Joe and another friend. Neda had been traveling for many hours. It was her first trip on a plane, and she was very sick most of the trip. She arrived exhausted. The following day, we went to Abilene and after Neda rested and went to a beauty salon, she looked far better and more relaxed.

After one month, on April 23, 1962, Joe and Neda were married in the First Baptist Church of Electra, Texas, thanks to my friends James and Sarah Totten who helped with all the wedding arrangements. Pastor Doyle Combs, a Baptist preacher and a friend of mine, performed the wedding and Sarah Totten was Neda's maid of honor.

Joe and Neda lived in the house on the farm, just outside Eastland. After the wedding, I completed my third year at the university. I was grateful that now my sister Neda was close by, and I could finally get some good Palestinian food!

During my four years at H-SU, several individuals and families meant much to me. One, Doyle Combs, was a young Baptist preacher. Although he was completing his studies for ministry at H-SU, he was already pastoring a Baptist church in the Abilene vicinity. He was also like a brother to me and many times I was invited to his home for a meal and fellowship. He introduced me to his wife and young children. One of the wonderful surprises that filled me with great joy was the time I visited the country church Doyle was pastoring, and he presented me with a very precious gift—a diatonic accordion. Doyle did not realize that his gift was a great investment in my future. This accordion has accompanied me throughout my ministry. I have used it for Sunday school, camps, church occasions, and celebrations. It is still with me. It is my priceless possession.

My First Encounter with Christian Zionism

A group of very active women from the First Baptist Church in Electra, Texas, had been sponsoring a group of "home kids" in Nazareth in the early 1950s. The Southern Baptist missionaries in Nazareth had gathered a group of nineteen children, mainly orphans, during the 1948 Israel/Palestine war. The American missionaries provided a home for them. After we went from Beisan to Nazareth, my sister Fida was employed as a house mother for these kids. Through their missionary network, the group of women in Electra had become aware that Fida's brother had just come from Nazareth to go to school at Hardin-Simmons University. They contacted the university and invited me to Electra to meet with them. One of the men whose wife was a member of the group came in their Cessna plane, picked me up from Abilene, and flew me to Electra where I stayed with James and Sarah Totten and their two small daughters. James was codirector of the Totten Funeral Home.

The women were Southern Baptists and active members of First Baptist Church in Electra. They were very dedicated believers and were led in regular Bible study by Mrs. Brian Jones. They met me with great warmth and kindness, and I felt almost adopted from the first minute. We gathered at Mrs. Jones's home over a potluck dinner. All the women with their spouses were there. I told them about Nazareth and the "home kids." I told them about my sister Fida and her work with the American missionaries. I also told them about my family background and about our being evicted from Beisan. That evening was extremely pleasant, getting to know them and answering their questions about Nazareth and Israel. I told them about the work of the Southern Baptist missionaries whom I had come to know firsthand. Some of them were my teachers at the Nazareth school. I also mentioned how I used to go every Sunday afternoon with the American missionaries to the village of Turan for Sunday school and mission work. Electra became a second home to me. I was invited multiple times to people's homes and their kind hospitality was superb.

It was in Electra with these wonderful women that I first heard the name of John Nelson Darby, an Irish Anglican priest who left the Anglican church and was credited with becoming the father of dispensationalism.[3] I heard words that I had never heard before, like premillennialism, postmillennialism, and amillennialism,[4] and I heard biblical interpretations that I had never known or imagined.

I thought I knew my Bible well. I had followed my father's method of reading the Bible. I used to complete reading the Old Testament once every year, and the New Testament twice a year. Admittedly, I would skip some of the boring stuff, but over the years, my knowledge of the content of the Bible was very good. Listening, however, to the way some of the friends in Electra were interpreting the text, mixing verses from the Old with the New Testaments, was puzzling and nonsensical. They were expressing theories and arriving at conclusions that seemed strange and odd to me. They believed that they were living in the end times and that the second coming of Christ was imminent. They mentioned that one of the clear signs of the end was the establishment of the state of Israel and the return and ingathering of Jews in Palestine. I tried politely to express a different position and to talk about God's justice and truth, but I felt that I did not know enough and was no match for the way they were linking verses together or for their way of interpreting the prophecies of the Bible and their insistence that the prophecies were being fulfilled in our time. I felt that I needed to study more about what they were talking about.

This was my first encounter with Christian Zionism at its core. I was in the presence of dedicated Christian believers who were committed to

3. Dispensationalism is an approach to biblical interpretation which states that God uses different means of working with people (Israel and the church) during different periods (dispensations) of history, usually seven chronologically successive periods.

4. Premillennialism is the view that Christ's return will usher in a future millennium of messianic rule mentioned in Revelation. Postmillennialism is the doctrine or belief that the second coming of Christ will follow the millennium. Amillennialism is the teaching that there is no literal one-thousand-year reign of Christ as referenced in Rev 20.

theories and interpretations that seemed strange to my ears. This was long before I had the benefit of theological education. Indeed, I loved these people, but in my heart and mind I felt something was terribly wrong with their interpretation of the biblical text.

It was years later, when Sabeel came into being, that I became increasingly aware of the influence and impact of Christian Zionism's false teaching on the politics of the Israel/Palestine conflict, having spent many hours studying the history, politics, and theology of Christian Zionism. Under this ideology, which was hidden under the cloak of legitimate theology, Palestinians were an inconvenience, expendable. Sabeel held an international conference on the subject in 2004. Dismantling Christian Zionism continues to remain a challenge for evangelicals in both the United Kingdom and the United States.

As a result of my visit to Electra, I was invited by James and Sarah Totten to work at their funeral home the following summer. After completing my second year of studies, the Tottens kindly came to the university and picked me up from the dormitory. I lived in their home for the summer and worked at the funeral home.

Working at the funeral home was an amazing experience that I could not forget. My work ranged from mowing the grass to driving the ambulance and the hearse to helping in the embalming of the dead. One of the dilemmas I faced was how to pray for my work. If I prayed, "God bless my work" or "God bless this business," it didn't sound right. I couldn't pray that way. Conversely, if I prayed, "God, don't bless this work," then I would lose my job. How should I pray? I reflected on this and finally decided that the best way to pray was: "God, I know that some people are going to die. Make them die in this area so we can get the business!"

The Totten's home became another place that I called home. As I alluded to before, they were very generous and helpful in arranging the details for Neda's wedding at their home church in Electra.

During my four years at Hardin-Simmons, there were many other families that invited me to their homes and showed me much kindness and hospitality. I was grateful for every one of them. I was also thankful to have been invited by the university chaplain to speak at the chapel services multiple times during my four years at the university. The first time was during my first year when I spoke about Nazareth where I had been raised. Another time that I still remember was when I won the E. P. Mead Speech

Contest at the university and was asked to recite my speech during the chapel service.

However, the response to my last speech, just before graduation, was less cordial. I was asked to speak about important impressions during my four years at Hardin-Simmons. I mentioned the kindness and generosity of the people of Texas who had made me feel at home, and the many friends that I had made. My last point had to do with the decision the university had made to finally admit black students. I had often wondered why I, a foreigner coming from across the world, would be accepted and admitted into the university while fully born Americans had been denied admission because of the color of their skin.

The next day, I received in my mailbox a note that read, "Mr. nigger lover, some of us did not appreciate what you said in chapel yesterday. Go back to your country. Signed: a discriminating white man." While the message shocked me, I knew that I had spoken the truth and was glad that I had been heard.

A short time later, on May 27, 1963, I graduated from Hardin-Simmons University, Abilene, Texas. The experience had opened my eyes to the sin of racism in another part of the world and would later help form my understanding of liberation theology. While my focus would be on Palestinian liberation from occupation and oppression, I was beginning to learn that liberation must be for all people everywhere.

I am thankful to God that I left Hardin-Simmons University a more inclusive place than when I came. And I was touched years later to be named a notable alumnus by the university. Others on the list include actors, athletes, and politicians.

On to Seminary

During my last year at Hardin-Simmons, I wrote to the Anglican archbishop in Jerusalem, Campbell MacInnes, to update him on my educational status. I mentioned that I would soon graduate from university and would be ready to go to seminary. He wrote back suggesting that it would be better if I attended seminary in England rather than in the United States. I replied that after four years in the States I had gotten used to the American system of education and would prefer to continue my seminary training there. I also mentioned that God had led me thus far and that I was certain that God would guide me into the next stage of the journey.

A few weeks later, I received a telephone call from Bishop James Pike, Episcopal bishop of the diocese of California in San Francisco, offering to help me with the choice of seminary. He mentioned that there was an Episcopal seminary in Austin, Texas. I explained that after four years in Texas, I would like to see another part of the country. He suggested the Church Divinity School of the Pacific (CDSP) in Berkeley, California, and I replied with a resounding, "Yes. I would love to come to California." Bishop Pike was very kind. He helped me connect with the Episcopal Church Center in New York for a scholarship, and I applied to Dean Sherman Johnson of CDSP for admission. I was thankful that all my applications and arrangements went very smoothly. The Episcopal Church Center granted me a full scholarship, and CDSP accepted me as a first-year seminarian for the 1963 fall semester.

Since my sister Neda was expecting her first child in August, I decided to wait until the baby was born before going to California. Shannon was born on July 10, 1963. I stayed a bit longer with Neda and then I boarded a Greyhound bus to Berkeley, California.

6

The Church Divinity School of the Pacific (CDSP)

THE GREYHOUND BUS DROPPED me off at the Shattuck bus stop in Berkeley, California, and a taxicab took me up the hill to the Episcopal seminary. I was welcomed by Sherman Johnson, the dean of the seminary. Dr. Johnson was a New Testament scholar and was well-known for his commentary on the Gospel of Mark in the Abingdon Bible Commentary. He was very familiar with Palestine and had visited East Jerusalem, long before the 1967 war, while working on an archeological dig at al-Jeeb (ancient Gibeon) in Jerusalem's vicinity.

I had arrived a few days before the fall semester started, so I spent my time familiarizing myself with CDSP and its surroundings. The seminary was located close to the north entrance of the University of California in Berkeley. A cluster of Christian seminaries were located nearby: Pacific School of Religion (PSR), Starr King Seminary (a Unitarian Universalist seminary), Jesuit School of Theology, Dominican School of Theology, and others. Years later, these and other seminaries formed the Graduate Theological Union (GTU) and were affiliated with the University of California, Berkeley.

I got good physical exercise walking on the campus of the university and by going up and down the hill to downtown Berkeley. The landscape was very different from the flat open plains of West Texas where I had spent the past four years.

There were around twenty-five seminarians in my freshman class. While most of them had recently graduated from university, many were older men (there was no women's ordination in those days) who were responding to a call for a change of vocation and a desire to serve God in the church. Some of them came with their families, and while the men went to seminary, most of the wives had day jobs to put food on the table. The children went to school.

Dean Johnson asked us to introduce ourselves. Alphabetically, I was one of the first. When we got to the letter "S," I heard the name Leonard Shaheen. I was very curious since Shaheen is an Arabic name. After we were dismissed, I went up to Leonard and introduced myself. He told me that his parents immigrated from Lebanon, but he was born in southern California. Leonard was married and had three children. Meeting Leonard started a long and wonderful friendship that lasted far beyond the three years of seminary.

Leonard became a strong advocate for justice for the Palestinians, and he and his wife, Julia, attended most of Sabeel's international conferences in Jerusalem. Leonard and Julia always came early to help us with the preconference preparations. Sadly, Leonard died prematurely in 2010, and a few months later, Julia unexpectedly followed him.

The first year in seminary was transformative for me. It was my life's dream come true. To actually be in seminary studying for the ordained ministry was my first concrete sign that after all these years, I found myself in the right place where I could receive the needed training to fulfill my call. Everything I had done so far in my life was in preparation and anticipation of this very moment. Here I was being prepared for my future ministry. It was exhilarating!

On the one hand, it was truly exciting to be in Berkeley, sitting at the feet of great scholars—giants like Sherman Johnson, Shunji Nishi, Massey Shepherd (a brilliant liturgical scholar who was an advisor to the Second Vatican Council), Sam Garrett (who unfolded the history of the church with such clarity and kindness), and others—and on the other hand, hoping and praying that God's will would be done in my life and ministry. I felt that God had led me to CDSP, and I put my full trust in God's providence and guidance. I was witnessing and experiencing God's answer to my persistent prayers ever since my childhood in Beisan.

What did I bring with me to seminary? What did I have to offer to God? I was bringing a deep conviction of God's call. I was bringing a simple childlike faith and trust that was nurtured by my father, mother, sisters, and brothers. I was bringing a good knowledge of the Bible that I had read regularly since childhood. I was bringing a mind that God had given me and that had been trained through university education to reason, think, analyze, deduce, and evaluate. I was humbly laying it all down before Christ with a prayer best expressed in the words of the hymn:

> Spirit of the living God, fall a-fresh on me.
> Melt me, mold me, fill me, use me.
> Spirit of the living God fall a-fresh on me.

My constant prayer was that through seminary education I could become equipped to serve God in Christ, in the church as well as outside the church, by serving my fellow human beings.

The first year was not easy. Theological education challenged much of my simplistic and superficial understanding of the Bible. It helped me to look deeper at the text of Scripture, to try to understand the message the writer wanted to communicate, to see how the first listeners and readers understood it, and to ask what the meaning of the message was for us today, i.e., how do we understand and apply it in our lives? It sifted and removed my latent literal and fundamentalist understanding of biblical texts and trained me to dig deeper in order to arrive at the essential meaning. This was not only true in the biblical courses, but it was even more rewarding in the study of theology, liturgy, and church history. My theological education was well rounded, stimulating, and maturing for me.

My theology courses were in systematics taught by Professor Shunji Nishi, who taught me how to think about God. I had little understanding of the different theological disciplines that were used to understand the nature of God, such as contextual theology and process theology, and, of course, at that time there was no such discipline as liberation theology. That would not emerge fully onto the scene until the publication of Gustavo Gutierrez's seminal book *Teología de la Liberación* in 1971. Many years later I would meet this great man whose work made possible my contribution to Palestinian liberation theology.

There was, however, another dimension to my education that I also greatly appreciated, although it was not clear to me at the time. Living and studying in Berkeley at the height of the civil rights movement was a continuing eye-opener for me, as my experience had been at Hardin-Simmons.

In 1964, the Free Speech Movement erupted among students on the campus of the University of California in Berkeley, just down the road from the seminary. The movement was inspired by the struggle for civil rights and later by opposition to the Vietnam War. Although I was not involved in the movement, I occasionally would go with my seminary friends to listen to some of the speeches that were given. I felt the spirit of the movement and its passion for justice. My general education expanded exponentially due to those experiences.

One other added blessing of my seminary days was the discipline of daily worship that included Holy Communion and hymn singing. Later in my parish ministry, I was always thankful for the theological education and experiences at CDSP that grounded me for all that was to follow.

Learning Sign Language

My seminary education afforded me several other formational opportunities to expand my worldview outside the world of academics. In my first year of study, I met Roger Pickering, who became a widely known priest in the church and who, along with his wife, championed a ministry with the deaf. Under Roger, I learned sign language and started helping him as much as I could. On a few occasions, I led morning prayer in sign language for the small group of deaf people who worshipped at St. Mark's Episcopal Church in Berkeley. Once, I asked one of the worshippers whether she was able to understand my signing. She said that she could, but I had an accent. I laughed because in both my speaking and signing I seemed to have an accent.

Ministry at Grand Canyon

After my first year at CDSP, I was accepted as a seminarian to spend a summer on the north rim of the Grand Canyon with an ecumenical organization called A Christian Ministry in the National Parks. It conducted worship services for tourists and visitors who came to visit from the States as well as from all over the world.

As soon as my first year in seminary ended, I took a Greyhound bus to Utah and from there followed the instructions that got me to the north rim of the Grand Canyon. I could not believe my eyes when I looked down at the canyon. It was a thrilling, breathtaking, and most magnificent sight.

I believe we had over 150 college students who had come to work in the park for the summer. Most of the students were Mormons because of the proximity of the north rim to the state of Utah, where Mormons made up the majority of the population.

I was assigned a job as a busboy in the lodge. This was going to be my regular paid job at the park. The Christian ministry part would be a wonderful training time for me in the service for Christ. In doing ministry at the north rim, I discovered that I had a Catholic and a Mormon counterpart. An added joy to the summer was the arrival of my younger brother, Saleem, who spent much of the summer with me, having moved to Texas to study after his graduation from high school. We enjoyed an incredible and memorable hike across the canyon floor.

Meeting Mormons

One of the exciting adventures was meeting Mormons for the first time in my life. I was fascinated by this new religion that I had not heard of. I started learning as much as I could about it. Some Mormons were eager to give me their holy books, which helped me understand them. One of the problems that arose that summer had to do with Mormon students who were trying to evangelize the Protestant students. I discussed this with my Catholic and Mormon friends, and we agreed to meet once a week for an open discussion where we would address one of the controversial topics from the three perspectives of our faith as Catholics, Protestants, and Mormons. Obviously, most of the time, the Protestants and the Catholics were on one side and the Mormons were on the other.

In the meantime, in my own study I had become quite knowledgeable about the differences in the doctrines and beliefs of the Mormons and how to counter them. In our public discussions, we were able to touch on our view and understanding of God, the Trinity, on Jesus Christ's life, the Bible, on baptism, and many other relevant topics. Every week we had very stimulating discussions that enriched our relationships and created synergy and vitality. One of the wonderful Mormon students I met was Colleen Germer. We became good friends, and I learned a great deal from her about Mormonism, its doctrines, beliefs, and ethics. Although I was impressed by the moral behavior of some of the Mormon students, it was difficult to accept the doctrinal basis of their beliefs. I found them contrary to the basic doctrines and tenets of the Christian church.

On my way back to Berkeley, Colleen was instrumental in introducing me to some of the Mormon officials at Salt Lake City, and I was given a special VIP visit to Mormon holy places, including the Tabernacle and the allowed parts of their Mormon temple. My time at the Grand Canyon with so many Mormons did indeed deepen my own faith, and I returned for my second year in seminary better prepared.

Piedmont Community Church

During my last year in seminary, I worked with high school students at Piedmont Community Church, an interdenominational and inclusive church in Oakland, California. My job entailed working with high school students, leading them in a form of worship, not necessarily formal, in the chapel on Sunday afternoons, and meeting with them every Wednesday for Bible study, discussion, and fellowship. My reflections touched on issues that were vital to their everyday life, and we always had plenty of time for thoughtful discussion. I was thankful that the level of friendship and trust deepened between us. They confided in me and became my younger brothers and sisters. I was thankful for the love, trust, and respect that united us. And the time was wonderful preparation for my future ministry.

One additional footnote to this rich experience was the generosity of the young people to raise money to buy me a car. Between their car washes and Bishop Pike's help, a black squareback Volkswagen was ordered from the factory in Frankfurt, Germany. It was arranged for me to pick it up at Frankfurt airport on my way back home.

Homeward Bound

On June 2, 1966, I graduated from CDSP with a master of divinity (MDiv) degree. Saleem and my mother attended my graduation. We drove back to Eastland, Texas, and stayed for a few weeks with Neda and Joe, and then my mother and I started our journey back home. We flew to Frankfurt, Germany, and were met by a man who had the papers for the car. I signed them and he gave me the keys. Mother and I had a good holiday, driving through the southern-German Black Forest, to Innsbruck, Austria, to Rome, and all the way south to Brindisi, Italy, staying in bed and breakfast places along the way. In Brindisi, we got on the boat and a few days later docked at Haifa seaport in Israel. My brother Michel and my sisters were all there to meet us. I was home! This homecoming coincided with the lifting of military law, which had been imposed on us since 1948. But this hopeful sign of a better future for Palestinians would quickly be dashed.

I was ordained a deacon in Christ Church, Nazareth, on October 16, 1966, by the Anglican Archbishop in Jerusalem, Campbell MacInnes. As I was kneeling before the altar praying, I looked up at the words of Jesus Christ written in beautiful Arabic calligraphy on the wall above the altar:

> The Spirit of the Lord is upon me,
> Because he has anointed me
> To bring good news to the poor.
> He has sent me to proclaim release to the captives
> and recovery of sight to the blind,
> to let the oppressed go free,
> to proclaim the year of the Lord's favor.
> (Luke 4:18–19)

I remembered my father, and gave thanks to God for him, and I was grateful that my mother was present in the church witnessing the blessing I was receiving through my ordination. My heart was full.

Seven months later, on May 21, 1967, at St. John the Evangelist Episcopal Church in Haifa, by the grace of God, I was ordained a priest. And thus, my boyhood dreams of being an Assis were fully realized. I also remember it was the hottest day of the year, a *khamsin*.[1]

But two weeks after my ordination to the priesthood, the 1967 war broke out. I was washing my car when my mother came out of the house and announced, "the war has started." I was numb. We had no idea what this war might portend for us. But we soon understood it would shatter the world of all Palestinians yet again. We were devastated by what followed. It would have the effect of another Nakba, not only resulting in the total occupation of Palestine including Jerusalem, but also the Golan Heights in Syria.

In the early days of the war, while I was driving to Nazareth, I passed Israeli army tanks and saw Israeli soldiers flashing the V sign. In anger I flashed the upside-down V sign. I was angry as Israel was quickly thrusting into Sinai and clearly winning the conflict and I was hoping that the war might liberate us. I could have been shot by those soldiers, but they moved on. But I remember my rage was overwhelming.

---

1. A *khamsin* is a dry, hot, at times sandy, local wind associated with a heat wave.

The Israeli air force, in a preemptive strike, completely destroyed the Egyptian and Syrian air forces, thus crippling their armies. Within a week Israel was able to occupy the Gaza Strip and the whole of the Sinai Peninsula, as well as the Golan Heights of Syria. With the defeat of the Jordanian army, Israel was then able to occupy the West Bank, including East Jerusalem. The Israel-Palestine conflict, which I had first experienced in Beisan, had just entered a stage of greater injustice and oppression, violence and bloodshed, and instability and insecurity that would mar the region for many years to come and continues as I write these words today. My ministry as an Assis and the oppression of my people were forever intertwined. A theology of liberation was unconsciously taking root within me.

7

My First Parish

Shefa Amer, Ibilene and Rameh

AFTER A WEEK OF rest in Nazareth at our family home, I was asked to take the worship service at St. Paul's Church in Shefa Amer, a town around twenty-two kilometers (thirteen miles) northwest of Nazareth. The congregation did not suffer any displacement during the 1948 war, but a large land area of the town had been confiscated in order to allow for the expansion of the Jewish town next to it.

At one time, Shefa Amer had a resident Episcopal minister but the last one had left to join his family in Jordan fourteen years before. During the first few weeks after my return home, I lead the worship services in a few churches on a temporary basis as I waited for the Majma to meet and assign me my charge. I also had to spend time studying classical Arabic since it had become quite rusty during my seven-year absence.

With my return home, we had, for the first time since the Nakba, four clergy to serve the ten Episcopal congregations in Israel. On October 16, 1966, three new clergy were ordained by Archbishop Campbell MacInnes: Rev. Bayouk Bayouk and Rev. Riah Abu-El-Assal were ordained priests, and I was ordained deacon. A few days later, the annual meeting of the Majma was held at Stella Carmel with the Rev. Khalil Duaybis, the head of the Majma, presiding, together with the archbishop and lay delegates from the various congregations. A number of crucial decisions were expected to be taken, especially the deployment of the three new clergy, none of whom took part in the deliberations. We awaited the decision of the Majma and eventually the results were announced in a plenary session. The Reverend Khalil Duaybis was moved from Nazareth to Haifa and was to resume his work as the head of the Majma. The Reverend Bayouk Bayouk was to serve the church in Kufur Yasif, the Reverend Riah Abu El-Assal the church in Shefa Amer, and I was assigned to Christ Church, Nazareth. This created a crisis for the Majma since Assis Riah wanted to serve Nazareth, which had the largest congregation in Israel after the Nakba, and he had been ordained a priest while I had just been ordained a deacon. This crisis was threatening the unity of the Majma.

This decision upset me. I went to see the archbishop privately and told him that I would be open to serving the church in Shefa Amer so that Riah could go to Nazareth. When the Majma's resolutions were going to be confirmed, the archbishop told the Majma that Naim would serve the church in Shefa Amer. Some of the delegates, including my brother Michel, who was one of them, were very upset with me for declining to go to Nazareth. But thank God, the crisis was diffused.

St. Paul's Episcopal Church in Shefa Amer had around 120 members when I became its pastor. The Majma rented a house for me in the town within walking distance from the church. I furnished it with my mother's help. It was wonderful that my mother decided to move from Nazareth and to come and look after me since I was still single. I started my ministry as a deacon in the fall of 1966. I was twenty-nine years old.

The Lord blessed the ministry in Shefa Amer. One of my first discoveries about St. Paul's Church was that almost every person in the parish had a God-given naturally beautiful voice. I attributed this, jokingly, to the water they drank.

Two elderly, dedicated, and pious men were of great help to me—Salim (Abu[1] Fuad) and Amin (Abu Aziz) Farah. Salim and Amin were brothers and retired businessmen. Amin was the father of Assis Rafiq and Assis Shafiq Farah. In the absence of a minister, Abu Fuad was a lay reader who used to lead the worship services in Shefa Amer and Kufur Yasif, just as my father had done in Beisan and Reineh. I often enjoyed sitting at their feet and listening to their stories and experiences in the church and in the Shefa Amer community.

One of the stories they related had to do with an elderly man from the Habiby family. In his old age, both his sight and hearing were lost but he never missed a Sunday without going to church. One day, a younger man

---

1. Abu is Arabic for "father of."

in the congregation asked him in a partly joking but exclamatory tone, "I cannot believe that you never miss a Sunday. You don't see and you don't hear. Why do you keep coming?" This wonderful old Christian got hold of this young man's shirt and gently shook him. "You're right, young man, I don't see, and I don't hear, but I come to church for those who can see and hear." What a wise saying!

With the help of Abu Aziz, I visited every family in my small parish. I inquired about their needs and wants. I tried to engage not only the father but equally the mother and the children. As the customs were, we couldn't leave without drinking a cup of Arabic coffee. I tried hard to limit my home visits to an hour but, unfortunately, it was difficult most of the time. I tried to tell people that I didn't drink coffee so that I wouldn't have to wait for it, but then they would insist on fixing tea, which was worse because it would take longer to drink. People's hospitality was amazing. Some of the families who had fruit gardens would bring me fruits in season, especially figs, cucumbers, apples, or plums.

In my experience as a pastor, pastoral visits were one of my most important activities. I did these on a regular basis, and I jotted down any special needs or concerns people had and tried to follow up with them. I always listened to people and gave them my full attention. I always prayed with them. I discovered that long after the pastor/minister leaves the parish, people judge him (there were no women clergy) by his pastoral care. Most members don't remember how great a preacher he was. They will remember, however, those times when he visited them, listened to their concerns and needs, prayed and stood with them in their time of need.

Counseling was another important ministry. There were several families as well as individuals who needed counseling. I was thankful that I had the advantage of taking more than one course in counseling at seminary and that was a tremendous help to me. On a few occasions, I counseled some people beyond my own church membership. After so many years of ministry, I still believe that one of the greatest needs in our diocese is the ministry of counseling. The need is great, and sadly we have not been able to meet this crucial need in a professional way.

In addition to my pastoral ministry in Shefa Amer, I discovered that our church had two families, the Musallams, living in the village of Ibiline, adjacent to Shefa Amer and seemingly forgotten. I went with Abu Aziz to visit them. It was a wonderful visit, and they were anxious for me to stay in touch. They were eager for me to hold a Sunday school for their children. In those days, it was more difficult to get to Ibiline because of the bad and winding road that went around the village. Since then, a new road has been built that has cut the distance considerably and made the village very accessible.

In order to establish the Sunday school in Ibiline, I decided to check with the Greek Catholic (Melkite) priest to see if he would be willing to allow me the use of their church hall. The Catholic priest was Elias Chacour, whom I had heard of but had not met before. I went to visit him and explained my need for a church hall to use for Sunday school for about ten children who belonged to my church. Father Chacour was gracious, and his answer pleasantly surprised me. He said, "You are welcome to use the church hall, provided you include in the Sunday school all the Catholic children." Every Sunday afternoon, I would take with me three teachers from St. Paul's Church, Sunday school material, and my diatonic accordion, and go to Ibiline. Instead of having ten children, we had over sixty children from the village.

That was the beginning of my friendship with Father Elias Chacour. Even after I left Shefa Amer four years later and moved to St. John the Evangelist in Haifa, our friendship remained solid. Many years later, when Sabeel came into being, Father Chacour was one of its founding members.

The Greek Catholic Church, i.e., the Melkite Church, was and continues to be the largest Christian church in Israel. When Archbishop Joseph Raya became the new bishop for the diocese of Acre, Haifa, and all Galilee at the end of the 1960s, there was great rejoicing and excitement among the tens of thousands of his parishioners. I was invited to his inaugural celebration at his See at St. Elias Melkite Church in Haifa. It was a great occasion, and the church was packed. For many of us, we saw in the new bishop a fresh prophetic voice that was sorely needed in the political stagnation in Israel. Archbishop Raya's words awakened within us a consciousness of the injustices inflicted upon our people and the need for liberation. They invoked in me a strong desire to pursue justice.

Before coming to assume his See in Haifa, Bishop Raya had spent seventeen years serving the Melkite church in Birmingham, Alabama, where he marched with Martin Luther King Jr. during the civil rights movement. He had seen laws of segregation between black and white. With this background, we were hoping that he would raise the voice of justice and liberation for the Palestinian people. In his sermon that morning, the bishop spoke well, although he had to show diplomatic shrewdness.

A few weeks later, Bishop Raya was invited to visit the large Melkite parish of Shefa Amer. It was an amazing celebration in the church and a big feast afterwards with boy scouts, drums, and bugles. It was my privilege to be asked to give a word of welcome on behalf of the various churches in the town. A few days later I was pleasantly surprised when Bishop Raya came to visit me at my home. This was an unexpected pleasure and made me very appreciative of his humble gesture. At the same time, it created a slight dilemma that was very awkward for me.

During my last year in seminary in Berkeley, I became aware of some medical studies that indicated the harmful effects of smoking. The pros and cons debates were still in their early stages at the time, but the evidence was quickly accumulating, showing a link between smoking and lung cancer.

When I returned home to Nazareth in the summer of 1966, I found that most people were still not aware of the dangers of smoking, and it was still part of the culture to have different brands of cigarettes set on a tray for people who came to visit. The host would immediately pick up the tray and offer the guests their choice of cigarette brands, and then he/she would light it for them.

I discussed this with my mother and told her that I would not offer cigarettes in my home. This was tantamount to giving people poison, and I would not do it. My mother argued that this had become part of our culture of offering hospitality. People expected it and if we didn't do it, some might accuse us of being stingy and culturally insensitive. It would be very embarrassing for us when people came to visit if we didn't offer them cigarettes. Mother suggested that we offer only one brand instead of four or five. I was not convinced. I told mother that I would provide ashtrays but not cigarettes.

When we moved to Shefa Amer to start my ministry, I did not provide any cigarettes to any visitor. Granted, it was embarrassing at first to watch people pull out a pack from their pocket and light a cigarette while I, the host, was sitting and watching. It was even more embarrassing when they offered their cigarettes to others in my house.

When I knew that Bishop Raya was coming to visit, the first thing that came to my mind was whether I should make an exception for the bishop, because I had seen him smoke when I was sitting next to him at the luncheon a few days before. My thoughts bothered me, but I decided not to make any exceptions.

The bishop arrived with his driver and another priest. My mother had prepared fresh lemonade with cake and coffee. In honor of the bishop's visit, I invited a few of our church elders. As soon as the bishop entered, one of the church elders pulled out his pack and offered the bishop a cigarette and lit it for him. It took some time for the feeling of embarrassment to subside but gradually it did. Soon it became clear in the church that Assis did not offer cigarettes at home. Slowly, people became aware of the dangers of smoking and an increasing number of people, yet not enough, stopped offering cigarettes in their homes.

I continued to be impressed by the presence of Archbishop Raya in our community. He focused much of his advocacy on two Christian villages, Iqrit and Kufur Birim, which had been forcefully evicted and the Israeli Supreme Court had ruled for their return.[2] He also embodied a nonviolent approach to the struggle we faced. He used nonviolent methods, sit-ins, demonstrations, and marches. No doubt he had seen these tactics during his days in the southern US civil rights movement. He had the courage to take a clear stand on behalf of the oppressed villagers. He was acting as their shepherd and protector.

I maintained my friendship with Bishop Raya even after I left Shefa Amer. I attended some of his seminars and visited him a few times in his Haifa residence. We enjoyed a few good discussions about the human and political rights of the Palestinians. I respected his passion for justice and the endeavors he undertook to create a movement for a just peace. Sadly, that did not materialize. I felt the spark that he ignited could have borne better results had it been more organized.[3] But his witness had inspired me to persevere with my own witness for justice. Eventually he resigned his See and left the country and retired in Canada. I was privileged to visit him twice in Canada, the last time a few months before his death.

A Ministry of Music

I alluded earlier to the fact that many of my parishioners in Shefa Amer were naturally gifted with beautiful voices. A few weeks after I got to meet and know the various families of the church, I announced in church that

---

2. Until this day these villages have not been allowed to return despite the Supreme Court's ruling.

3. Ateek, *Cry Out*, 24–28.

I would like to start a choir and invited all those who would like to join. Around twenty-five people showed up, both men and women.

As I mentioned earlier, after we moved to Nazareth, I started taking piano lessons from Sister Archangela of St. Joseph Catholic Order. Later, I took lessons from a professional piano teacher in Haifa. In Abilene, a Texas Baptist church organist offered me piano lessons for a year. So, I felt confident about starting a choir, but I had no experience in leading or conducting. I had to teach myself how to do that.

I started teaching the choir new hymns, and through them we were able to teach the whole congregation. We had an old pump organ in the church, and we used it well. In the absence of an organist, I was my own organist. With the choir leading the congregation, it was a joy to listen to the people sing. It literally revolutionized our worship services. The second stage was to go into singing in parts, but none of the members knew how to read music. I gave them a few simple lessons on how to follow the notes. I divided them into the four parts and started to teach every group to memorize their own part. When we put the four voices together, it was like discovering paradise.

Thus, began the Shefa Amer church choir. It was a great blessing whenever the choir sang in four voices during the church worship. We had good acoustics in the church and when the choir sang, the sound was truly amazing, and God was glorified. We started thinking how to share this God-given talent with our other churches. By the grace of God, I composed a special service of readings and songs. I asked one of our church members who had a wonderful reading voice to be the narrator and in between the readings, the choir sang in unison as well as in parts. With the help of some church volunteers, we built choir risers and organized multiple tours that included our churches in Nazareth, Kufur Yasif, Reineh, Nablus, Ramallah, as well as St. Andrew's Church of Scotland in Jerusalem. In Jerusalem, the program was video recorded by the Arab Israeli television service and later shown on public TV.

There was another objective I was hoping the choir could reach. Most of the hymns in our Arabic hymnal were imported to us through the Western Protestant missionaries who came to Palestine, Lebanon, and Syria in the nineteenth and twentieth centuries. What the early Arab Christian converts to Anglicanism and Presbyterianism did was to translate the Western hymns into Arabic and use the same Western tunes. In a few instances, our Arabic hymnal contained Arabic tunes put to Arabic poetry. Most frequently, however, some well-known Arab Christian writers and poets used Western tunes for their poems. I wanted to do the reverse. I stripped many Arabic hymns from their Western tunes and gave them popular, beautiful, though largely secular, Arabic tunes. This type of adaptation was within my reach with the help of my choir members who provided me with the Arabic tunes. Once we succeeded, we found within our church several members who played the needed musical instruments—the Oud,[4] violin, tambourine, and a *durbakkeh*.[5] We started practicing together using the well-known Arabic tunes that we were able to adapt to the hymns. When the choir started singing those hymns with the Arabic tunes, it was magic. It was easy to feel the liveliness and vivaciousness of the singers and their natural identification and affinity with the local music.

The main problem we encountered had to do with the fact that many of our church members associated the Arabic tunes with secular and non-spiritual things, while they associated the Western church tunes with sacred music, piety, and spirituality. Nevertheless, I was determined to introduce our people to a new spirituality that stemmed from our culture, ethos, and way of life. I continued to adapt spiritual hymns to popular secular tunes even after I left Shefa Amer and was assigned to St. John the Evangelist Episcopal Church in Haifa. The epitome of adapting hymns and songs to Arabic tunes was best expressed, a few years later, when I was able, by the grace of God, to organize a concert at St. John's in Haifa. It was an ecumenical occasion attended by all the heads of the churches in Haifa and hundreds of their church members. The Shefa Amer church choir was joined by our Haifa church choir in a celebration of Christian songs set to popular Arabic tunes. The Melkite and Maronite priests expressed publicly their appreciation. The whole event was innovative and groundbreaking. It was one of the great highlights of my ministry.

Although we had very few resources at the time, the enthusiasm of the Shefa Amer church choir members, their natural talent and its use for the glory of God was most inspiring to me, to their families, and to many others.

In one of my pastoral visits in Shefa Amer, I met a high school student from Haifa who was studying piano with a professional piano teacher who taught at the Conservatory of Music in Haifa. Her name was Mrs. Gruber. She mentioned that Mrs. Gruber was not only a very good teacher, but she also did not discriminate against any of her students. On the contrary, she

---

4. The Oud is a lute, a plucked string instrument very popular in the Middle East.

5. The durbakkeh or darabukka is a Middle East Arabic drum.

was very gracious and kind, especially toward her Arab Israeli students. I jotted down Mrs. Gruber's name and her phone number.

I contacted her and explained my ministry in Shefa Amer and my desire to have children learn to play the piano. I shared with her my hope to discover some hidden musical talents in the town. After our conversation, Mrs. Gruber started to come once a week on the bus from her Israeli Jewish town near Haifa to Shefa Amer to teach a few children and even some adults.

Mrs. Gruber was a German Jew who had escaped Hitler's concentration camps due to the love and kindness of her Christian neighbors. She promised herself to return that love and kindness to Christians who were hurting from discrimination and oppression. I believe she married a German Christian who lived his faith secretly among the Jewish community and when he died, he was buried in our Christian cemetery in Haifa.

Mrs. Gruber was an amazing person with a great love in her heart. She was truly loved by her students in Shefa Amer and was able to discover many wonderful talents among them. A couple of her students went on to the Jerusalem Conservatory of Music for further study. One of them, after completing her studies, went back to Shefa Amer and worked as a piano teacher. When we started this project, there was to my knowledge only one piano in the whole town. I served the church in Shefa Amer for almost five years, and when I left, the sound of pianos could be heard in multiple homes all over town.

Personal Tragedy Strikes

During the period of my ministry in Shefa Amer, two personal events impacted me deeply and severely. The first was the death of my oldest brother, Michel. After the 1967 war, my brother was diagnosed with leukemia. After the tragedy of our forced eviction from Beisan, Michel had become a successful goldsmith/jeweler in Nazareth. His sudden illness hit me very hard, and I could not share the bad news with his wife, nor did I dare mention it to my mother or any of my siblings. The burden was unbearable and unbelievable. His five children were still young. Nawal, his oldest daughter was thirteen years old, and his youngest son, Jeries, was only three. Michel went to the Nazareth Hospital for a blood test. When the results came back to Dr. Tester, the hospital director, whom I knew well, sent after me and told me the bad news. He suggested that I take Michel to Haifa to be examined by a hematologist. It was not easy to convince Michel to go with me to Haifa, but he did. In those days, it was not acceptable culturally to share a bad prognosis with the sick person or his family. People waited and slowly divulged the truth. The hematologist at the Rambam hospital confirmed that Michel had leukemia. When I asked him about the prognosis, he answered, from two to six months. It was as if someone had hit me in the face with a sledgehammer. What should I say to Michel? What could I say to the family? I asked the Lord for help. I told Michel that he had to be on strong medication for a while.

It was providential that during the few previous months since my return from the States, I had come to know a young American doctor who was sent by the Mennonites to work at the Nazareth Hospital. Dr. Bob Martin seemed to be a good doctor professionally. He was also very kind and gracious, and we had become friends. He was overseeing Michel's condition.

After a few weeks at home, Michel had to go into the Nazareth Hospital. His health began to steadily deteriorate. It was clear that the end was approaching. I sat with his wife, Wadi'a, and told her that Michel's condition was very serious. Sometime later, I told my mother and sisters. The time came when Michel went into a coma. As I sat in the room next to his bed, I was reciting some of the psalms and praying with him. I also started preparing my sermon for his funeral. On Monday, November 27, 1967, Michel died and went to be with the Lord. He was forty-four years old. Even now, when I am writing these words after over fifty years, I cannot help myself from crying. It was the biggest personal tragedy to hit our family.

Tested by Fire

The second difficult and bitter event was different, but its severity almost cost me my ministry, my life's work. The death of my brother took place toward the beginning of my ministry in Shefa Amer, while the second happened toward the end.

It began when I returned to the States in the summer of 1970 on my first visit since graduation. I took my one-month summer vacation to visit my sister Neda and Joe and their family and my brother Saleem, who was already doing graduate work at Baylor University. Saleem gave me his car and I drove to California to visit friends. While there, I met a woman, and it was love at first sight (or so it seemed). I rationalized my relationship and my love for her. I convinced myself that this could be the will of God for me.

Since my return home in 1966, I had tried my best to meet an Arab Palestinian woman, and my wonderful sisters had introduced me to some, but I had not felt attracted to any of them. I used to pray daily that God would guide me to the right person. My sisters would accuse me of setting the bar too high, but I always replied that I wanted a person who could both complement and supplement my ministry. The ministry of Christ had always been my highest calling, and the loftiest aspiration I hoped to attain.

I was, therefore, looking for a person with a college education (in those days, this was not easy to find in Israel/Palestine). I was looking for a person who had a good Christian background and was attracted by the church's ministry. I was hoping to find someone who loved music. I was searching for a person with a nice personality who loved people and enjoyed giving hospitality. I knew I was not perfect, but serving Christ was a special vocation and I wanted someone who could share that vocation with me.

When I decided to take a holiday and to return to the States in the summer of 1970, I was tired and exhausted from not finding the right person. I was disheartened and discouraged. My prayers expressed this despondency as I argued with God. Why can't I find the right person? I need to be married. Please, help me, Lord.

When I met this woman, I was attracted to her because I found in her some of the qualities I was looking for, but I was blinded to other essential things that could hinder my ministry among my people.

A few months after I returned home, she came to visit me in Shefa Amer, and we got engaged. My mother and a few of my siblings attended. Although I looked happy, deep down in my heart it was not what I had hoped for. Similarly, my mother and my sister Hilda were not happy at all. I took my fiancée on a visit to the holy and historical places before she returned home. In all our discussions, we vacillated between ministry in my country and ministry in the States. I always insisted on my original call to serve Christ in my home country, while she painted a rosy picture of ministry in the States where her father could facilitate things for us.

The inner struggle between the two ministries started mounting after she returned home. Several weeks later I took part in a retreat on Mount Carmel. I spent most of the night in agony and prayer. I was wrestling with two strong forces within me. The first force was God's call that went back to my early childhood in Beisan when I felt Christ's call to follow him. The call had never wavered and through the power of this call I had been able to withstand many temptations and was able to overcome them. I had spent seven years through university and seminary in the States. I had encountered multiple opportunities and enticements to stay. Why not stay and serve Christ in the States? It was the same Christ after all.

Such temptations were not strong enough to lure me. By the power of Christ, I was able to defeat them all. But then, suddenly, I was confronted by a power that weakened my resolve. It was a betrayal of the main purpose of my life. It was an infidelity on my part against the primary objective that God called me for. The wrestling went on for hours. I was literally in agony and tears. I still remember it well. I prayed for God's mercy and grace; I prayed for the Holy Spirit to guide me in making the right decision. That night, on top of Mount Carmel, I decided to break the engagement and to honor Christ's original call to me and to continue my ministry in my country, no matter what the cost might be. I felt tested by fire, but the good Lord stood by my side and strengthened me. Now that I had made the decision, I needed guidance to carry it through.

Instead of writing to my fiancée, I felt that the honorable way was to go back to the States and discuss it with her and her parents in person and explain my position about the importance of ministry in my homeland.

In those days, we did not have an indigenous Arab/Palestinian bishop in Jerusalem. I went to see Archbishop George Appleton and requested a year's leave for further study. He gave me his blessing. In the summer of 1971, I ended my ministry in Shefa Amer and flew back to the States for one year's sabbatical. My mother left Shefa Amer and went back to her home in Nazareth.

At the dinner table that first evening after my arrival, I explained my position to my fiancée and her parents, hoping they would understand. I did not imagine that it was going to infuriate them. I was showered with insults and name-calling; I was never humiliated as much as I was that night, and I was asked to leave the house.

I took a Greyhound bus and traveled to the Church Divinity School of the Pacific in Berkeley, California. It took some time to recuperate and find healing and peace from the awful trauma that I had experienced. The fall semester at the Graduate Theological Union (GTU) was about to start. I took multiple refresher courses, including courses for counseling at Pacific School of Religion (PSR) since I felt its great need for my pastoral ministry. In fact, I completed enough courses for another master's degree, but I did not submit a thesis.

During that year, I used to worship at All Soul's Episcopal Church down the road from the seminary and assist its wonderful first African American priest. When the priest decided to leave All Soul's and return to Chicago, the vestry asked me to fill in as the Locum Tenens. I felt it was providential, and I thankfully accepted. For over two months I served that parish. One Sunday after the morning worship, I was greeted at the door in Arabic by a Palestinian woman who was visiting her daughter in Berkeley. They invited me for coffee that afternoon. Mrs. Amy Aranki and her daughter Abla were members of the small St. Peter's Episcopal Church in Birzeit, Palestine, near Ramallah. We had a good visit. I did not know then that Mrs. Aranki had another daughter, Maha, who was studying at Beirut University College in Lebanon, and that in two years, Mrs. Aranki would be my mother-in-law.

At the end of the summer, it was time for me to return home. All Soul's Vestry asked me whether I would consider staying, but without any hesitation, I said that I had a commitment to return and resume my ministry with my people. I packed my few belongings and returned home.

8

Ministry in Haifa, Ramleh, Lydda, and Acre

IN THE SUMMER OF 1972, I returned home full of enthusiasm to resume my ministry in my homeland. I was grateful to God that the heavy burden I'd left with had dissipated, and the reality of Christ's call had returned to me refreshed and reinvigorated. I felt restored and reenergized.

Before my return, the Majma, in its annual meeting, had assigned me to serve St. John the Evangelist Church in Haifa. I moved to the first floor of a two-story church building in St. Luke's Compound. Culturally, it was a blessing that my mother was able to leave her home in Nazareth where she had been living and come to live with me.

Under the British Mandate, before the Nakba, Haifa had a very active Anglican ministry. There were two Anglican churches. One was St. John's, with its Palestinian pastor serving the local Palestinian congregation. It was the largest Anglican/Episcopal church in the whole of Palestine with a membership that exceeded a thousand people. Most of its members were considered the elite of society—businesspeople, lawyers, judges, engineers, doctors, educators, etc. The church also ran a primary school for Arab children.

On the English side, St. Luke's Anglican Church had its own British chaplain who served a resident British community. In addition, there was St. Luke's School for boys and an English high school for girls that served the Haifa community and vicinity. Palestinians and Jews lived together, and quite peaceably, in this beautiful city. Sometimes, the mayor of Haifa was a Palestinian, other times, Jewish. Haifa had multiple consulates including British and French as well as others.

The Palestinian Nakba changed everything. When Haifa fell, on April 23, 1948, about seventy thousand Palestinian Arabs were forced out and directed to the port to flee to Lebanon. Those who stayed, about 350, were forced to live in the controlled section of Wadi Nisnas. Most of the affluent people of Haifa fled by boat to Beirut, Lebanon, hoping to return when the violence subsided. Others went to Nazareth and could not return to their homes in Haifa. Most people's lives were totally disrupted. Our church in Haifa can serve as a good illustration of the drastic upheaval that took place when Haifa fell into Zionist hands. As already mentioned, our church had a membership that exceeded a thousand people. After the Nakba, only sixty people remained, most of them from the working class.

By the time I came to Haifa in 1972, St. Luke's British ministry had dwindled. There was still a British chaplain but most of the congregation had left. Finally, the chaplain himself left. I continued to hold a Holy Communion service for a handful of English-speaking people for a few months, but when they left Haifa, I stopped. I started using St. Luke's Church for our Palestinian congregation because its size was appropriate for our diminished numbers. We only used the large St. John's Church on feast days.

During the Nakba, St. John's school in Haifa closed. In 1950, Assis Rafiq Farah opened the school with twenty-one children. Gradually, the school reached the seventh grade with 250 students. For several years, Assis Rafiq was the only minister looking after the remnant church communities in what became Israel. In 1965, however, Assis Rafiq and his family decided to move to the West Bank, which was, at the time, under Jordan. Later, he became the minister of two churches, St. Andrew's Episcopal Church in Ramallah and nearby St. Peter's Episcopal Church in Birzeit.

One of the first things I did as the minister of St. John's was to visit the church families. The number of the congregation had increased to almost two hundred. My ministry covered the gamut of pastoral care, including preaching and teaching. I spoke at the school's chapel and led the students in songs using my diatonic accordion. I also met with the teachers on a regular basis. St. John's was very fortunate to have Naji Farah and later Akram Haddad as its principals. Both were good and respected educators, and under their leadership St. John's primary school fared well in the Haifa

Arab community. Most of our graduates continued their high school at the Orthodox College (high school) in town. One of the greatest problems I encountered had to do with teachers' salaries. The school did not receive external support from the Ministry of Education (now it does) and the collected fees were not enough. In spite of this perennial problem, the school had the benefit of wonderful and dedicated teachers who gave the students the best education possible.

By the grace of God, in addition to the regular worship services and the Sunday school for children, it was possible to organize a vibrant pastoral care ministry through the pastorate committee visits, as well as the women's activities and visits to family church members. As I did in Shefa Amer, I organized a church choir in Haifa. We had some good singers and, occasionally, the two choirs performed together. In 1984, when Assis Samir Kafity was installed as the bishop in Jerusalem, the two choirs united and led the singing at his inauguration in St. George's Cathedral, Jerusalem.

The Ecumenical Ministry

When I think about my ministry in Haifa, one of the things that stands out is the ecumenical dimension that, I believe, flowered by the power of the Holy Spirit. It all started when I decided to meet the priests of the other churches in the city, namely, the Greek Catholics (Melkites), the Greek (Byzantine) Orthodox, the Roman Catholics (Latin), and the Maronites. I started with Abuna Botros Haddad and Abuna Michel Zammar, the priests of the Melkites, the largest church in Haifa. Both were Lebanese. Abuna Botros was an elderly man, godly and pious, and a scholar of Eastern church liturgy.

I shared with him my thoughts on bringing together all the local clergy for regular meetings and letting the Holy Spirit guide us in bringing the Christian community closer together. I was frank with the priest. I asked him if he would be willing to be our moderator; I would be glad to act as the secretary for the group and do the organizing work. And so, it happened. He called all the clergy, and we began meeting regularly and soon we became friends, brothers, and servants of the Christian community in Haifa. Later, I was thankful that they welcomed Rev. Ibrahim Simaan, the Baptist pastor in town.

As Christmas was approaching, and on behalf of the Christian clergy of Haifa, I wrote to the city mayor and requested that the municipality decorate with multicolor lights the big eucalyptus tree at the entrance of Wadi

Nisnas, where most of the population was Arab. To our great surprise, the mayor wrote back and promised to do it. That was the beginning. From then on, every year, the large tree was lit up for Christmas and other trees began to be lit by the residents.

Another development was the exchanging of pulpits. In order to reflect our unity in Christ, we agreed to preach in each other's churches. This action sent a very strong and clear message to our people that we were one in Christ, and that we loved and respected the other churches as we loved and respected our own. An example of this ecumenical spirit was when, for multiple years, the Roman Catholic priest would come to help me serve communion on feast days. At that time, the laity were not allowed to help serve communion and it would take me a long time to serve the bread first and then the wine to all those who came to partake. The Latin priest agreed to come and help me. Such an act was revolutionary for most of our members.

On more than one occasion, we filled several buses with our people from the various churches and took them to the Sea of Galilee where we visited the holy sites and connected them with the life of our Lord Jesus Christ and our ministry today. Every place we visited, we read the appropriate gospel story and commented on it. Those visits were amazingly transformative for our Christian community in Haifa. In fact, the visit to the Sea of Galilee was the climax of a several months' study course we conducted on the life and ministry of Jesus. Such activities brought a spiritual revival to many Christians within the Haifa community. People started to meet and relate to each other in a new ecumenical way. On Maundy Thursday, after the worship service at night, groups from every church visited the other churches for a time of prayer, meditation, and adoration of Christ's passion. We felt the Spirit of Christ among us, guiding and blessing us. These were the seeds of a future vision of ecumenism.

Church of Ramleh

In addition to my ministry in Haifa, I was assigned the ministry of our Emanuel Church in Ramleh. Every Sunday afternoon, I would drive over sixty miles to Ramleh for an early evening worship service. Often, I used to spend the night at Saalem Fanous's home and then return to Haifa the following day. Years later, one of Saalem's sons, Samuel, went to Virginia Theological Seminary, where he received his training for the ministry and was ordained as an Episcopal priest and served a number of churches in our Jerusalem Diocese.

At Ramleh I started a ministry for young people, and God blessed the meetings. When we started, we had no place to meet except in the church's cemetery adjacent to the church. Later, we were able to build a simple structure that gave us shade and privacy. We had almost forty young men and women who met regularly, and one of the Fanous brothers, Sim'aan (an older brother of Samuel), was in charge of organizing and coordinating the activities. It was an amazing group of young people who belonged to the various churches of Ramleh. The activities included Bible study, discussions of relevant topics that related to everyday life, a big hike to the Latrun Monastery, and an amazing New Year celebration, which we held in Lydda. It was a joy to be with them. I served the church in Ramleh from 1972 to 1977.

Meeting Maha

One Saturday afternoon, while I was preparing for our Sunday service in Haifa, I received a phone call from Assis Rafiq Farah, the minister of our two churches in Ramallah and Birzeit on the West Bank. He wanted to introduce me to a parishioner who had recently arrived from Beirut, Lebanon, having completed her bachelor of arts degree. "Her name is Maha Aranki, and she is a member of our church in Birzeit and is already playing the organ for us." He added, "Maha comes from a very good church family, and I'd like you to meet her. If you'd like, you can join me next Monday on a pastoral visit and meet the family."

On Sunday, I drove in the afternoon, as usual, to Ramleh and conducted the worship service at our Emanuel Church. Then I drove to Jerusalem and spent the night with my sister Hilda's family. On Monday, as agreed, I met Assis Rafiq in Ramallah and both of us went in the afternoon to Birzeit on a pastoral visit to the Aranki family. As soon as we entered the house, I recognized that Maha's mother, Amy (Em[1] Suhail), was the woman I'd met a year before with her daughter Abla at All Soul's Episcopal Parish in Berkeley, California, where I was serving as Locum Tenens. What an amazing coincidence! Later, I believed it was providential.

Assis Rafiq introduced me to the family, Maha's father, Fuad (Abu Suhail), Amy (Em Suhail), Maha, and her younger brother Sary. They welcomed us warmly. I started by asking Em Suhail about her visit to the

1. Em is Arabic for "mother of."

States. I then asked Abu Suheil about his work with UNRWA[2] in Jerusalem. We talked about their children. Suhail was living in London and working at the BBC while finishing his PhD in computer science. Osama was living in Houston, Texas, and working for Continental Airlines. Abla was living in San Francisco and working for the Federal Reserve Bank, and Sary was studying medicine at the American University in Beirut (AUB). Maha talked about her time at Beirut University College, where she'd studied. She also mentioned how every Sunday she attended All Saints Episcopal Church for worship. As Maha was talking, I sensed a deep feeling telling me, this is the woman you have been waiting for.

Maha served us coffee, and we stayed for about an hour. It was a good and enjoyable parish visit. We said goodbye and left. As we were walking to Assis Rafiq's car, he asked me, "What do you think?" I said, "I feel this is the right person for me. I hope to God that Maha is the person I have been waiting for. I would like to get to know her better."

I picked up my car from Ramallah, thanked Assis Rafiq, told him that I would be in touch with him, and drove home to Haifa. On the way back, I prayed for guidance. I prayed that God's will would be done. My mother was anxiously waiting for my return. I told her how I felt about Maha when I first laid eyes on her, but at this early stage, I felt that we needed to pray that God's will would be done.

A few days later, I got in touch with Assis Rafiq and asked him to arrange with Abu Suhail for me to go visit them again the following Monday. When I arrived at the house, Abu Suhail was sitting on the veranda. After a few minutes of small talk, I asked his permission to speak privately with Maha.

Maha and I went into the living room. I did not waste any time. I told her about my ministry and that ever since I was a small child, I'd felt God's call. I talked about my family background, my education, and my love for serving Christ. I mentioned that it had been difficult for me to meet someone who I felt could share ministry with me.

I added that from what Assis Rafiq had told me about her and her family, it seemed that she possessed certain qualities that were important for the ministry of the church. Therefore, I wanted to get to know her better so that both of us could determine whether we were good for each

2. United Nations Relief and Work Agency. Following the 1948 Arab-Israeli conflict, UNRWA was established by United Nations "General Assembly Resolution 302 (IV)" of December 8, 1949, to carry out direct relief and works programs for Palestine refugees. The Agency began operations on May 1, 1950.

other. I also elaborated about the blessings as well as the challenges of ministry, and I assured Maha that with God's help it was possible to overcome those challenges.

Maha shared with me her background, her family, her faith, and her connection to the church. Throughout the time we spent talking together (probably close to one hour), I was feeling good about our frank discussion and was hoping that she was feeling the same way.

To my utter disappointment, Maha made it clear that she did not share the same feelings and interest. We ended our meeting. I thanked her father for his kindness in allowing me to have a private conversation with Maha. I left Birzeit and returned to Haifa. That was the most agonizing trip of my life. All during the drive back, and for the next week, I wrestled with God. Why? After all these years, when I finally found the person that I felt was right for me and my ministry, she said no. I had been praying and waiting for many years and I felt that God had finally led me to this family and introduced me to Maha, only to discover that she did not share the same feelings and interest I had for her.

When I arrived home in Haifa, I shared the disappointing news with my mother. The rest of that week I felt great anguish and distress. Yet, in my heart, I still felt that Maha was the right person for me, and I could not drive her out of my mind. On Saturday, at the suggestion of my mother, I got in touch with Assis Rafiq and told him that Maha had said no, but I wondered whether she was open to reconsider.

On Sunday, just before the worship service started at Birzeit church, Assis Rafiq asked Maha whether she had second thoughts, and she said, yes. She told Assis Rafiq that she was thinking about it all week and she would like to see me again. I was overjoyed when Rafiq told me. On Monday, the next day, I drove back to Birzeit, and we sat together and talked. I went out to the veranda and told her father and mother that we had come to a basic understanding, and that we trusted God to be our guide and may God's will be done.

On September 2, 1973, in the presence of Bishop Najib Cub'ain and his wife, Assis Rafiq Farah, my mother, my uncle Kamel Karnik, my sister Hilda from Jerusalem, and Maha's parents, her brother Sary, and a few relatives from her side, Maha and I were engaged in her family home. Bishop Najib Cub'ain officiated.

Intentionally and significantly, I had chosen the second of September as the date for our engagement. Since my father, Stifan, had died on

September 2, 1960, when I was an undergraduate student at Hardin-Simmons University in Texas, I wanted to replace the date that gave my family much sorrow with a day that now gives us much joy.

For the next ten months, after the Sunday evening worship service in Ramleh, I would drive to Ramallah and spend the night with Assis Oudeh Rantisi at the Evangelical Boys' Home. On Monday mornings we usually had breakfast together at a small restaurant that served a dish of beans (*fool* in Arabic), which Oudeh and I enjoyed very much. On Monday afternoons, I would wait until Maha finished teaching at the Ramallah Girls' High School. I would pick her up and we would spend several hours together before I drove back to Haifa. Although our time together was brief because both of us were working and we were living over seventy miles apart, our getting together every Monday was one of the most enjoyable and precious times of our engagement days.

By the grace of God, on Sunday, July 7, 1974, we were married at St. George's Cathedral in Jerusalem. I was thankful that two busloads of people, one from Haifa and the other from Nazareth and Shefa Amer, came to the wedding. The combined choir of Haifa and Shefa Amer led the singing. Bishop Najib Cub'ain married us and several clergy took part in the ceremony, including Canon Fayek Haddad (later Bishop Haddad), Archdeacon Rafiq Farah, and Rev. Ronald Metz.

Having the wedding in Jerusalem made it easier for Maha's family and their friends and relatives from Birzeit and Ramallah to attend. I was thankful to God for the blessings of my marriage to Maha and for her wonderful Aranki family.

Providentially, the church in Haifa had a large house with two floors. This made it possible for mother to stay living in her room on the first floor. The rest of the space was used by the church as a Christian family center where we met for coffee after church and where we had some of our church meetings and activities. Maha and I lived on the second floor where, years before, the British chaplain had lived.

The Struggle for Indigenous Leadership

During my ministry in Haifa, I became involved, with other clergy colleagues, in the discussion between the Archbishop of Canterbury and our standing committee and church council (Majma) over the question of the bishopric of Jerusalem.[3] In 1905, the Arab Evangelical Episcopal Church Council (AEECC) came into being. The Church Missionary Society (CMS) was the main mission agency through which the Holy Spirit was active in the establishment of the new church community in Palestine and Jordan. It took fifty-three years for us to have our first Arab bishop. It was on January 6, 1958, when Archbishop MacInnes consecrated Canon Najib Cub'ain as the Bishop of the Diocese of Jordan, Lebanon, and Syria. This new diocese did not include the state of Israel. Due to political considerations, Israel remained under the direct jurisdiction of the British Archbishop.

Such an ecclesiastical arrangement reflected a prolonged and serious discussion between the Archbishop of Canterbury and the nascent Arab Evangelical Episcopal Church (AEEC) that went back many years. My first serious encounter with this issue took place in the 1970s when Canon Howard Root was sent by the Archbishop of Canterbury to continue the discussion on the form and shape of the provincial structure of the Episcopal Church in the Middle East. Canon Root and I spent quality time together discussing this topic with candor and truthfulness. I challenged the idea that the Archbishop in Jerusalem must be British because of the special status of Jerusalem. I insisted that in the Anglican Church, the locally elected bishop should be the official representative of the Anglican Communion.[4]

This was the most critical sticking point in the discussion. Obviously, the discussion was complicated by political issues of Israel's occupation of Palestine. Some people argued that the presence of a British bishop could have greater clout vis-à-vis the Israeli government that might have positive consequences for the lives of the indigenous Arab Anglicans living under occupation. Some of us countered that there were no guarantees for that. On the contrary, it might be detrimental. Let the church be the church, standing up and struggling for its own rights vis-à-vis the political powers. Canon Howard Root met with various people and submitted his report to the Archbishop of Canterbury.

After the retirement of Archbishop Campbell MacInnes in 1968, Archbishop George Appleton was appointed with the mandate to prepare the church for self-government. In his sermon during his installation at

---

3. Assis Rafiq Farah has covered the essence of those discussions in his book, *In Troubled Waters.*

4. The Anglican Bishop *in* Jerusalem and not *of* Jerusalem because we recognize that the Bishop of Jerusalem is the Greek Orthodox Patriarch.

St. George's Cathedral on Sunday March 23, 1969, Appleton emphasized the importance of church unity and the work of peace and reconciliation. He added that the achievement of peace requires a commitment to truth and justice.

Archbishop Appleton had a passion for peacemaking and reconciliation. During his five years in Jerusalem, most of his energy was spent on praying and working for peace between Israelis and Palestinians. He, I am sure, believed that working for peace takes priority over ecclesiastical church structures. He was a kind and pious bishop and most of us clergy related well to him. However, he did not totally comprehend the complexity of the political situation and lacked the ability to make a dent in the struggle for peace.

During his stay in Jerusalem, in 1969, he appointed Rev. Peter Schneider and me as chapter canons of St. George's Cathedral. This appointment did not involve moving to Jerusalem from Haifa. Peter was born of Jewish parents in Europe. He became a Christian and was ordained a priest and his main ministry was focused on Jewish-Christian relations. The fact that he was made a canon was a good gesture on the part of the archbishop and did not raise any eyebrows. What did not go well with some Arab clergy was the fact that I was made a canon. I had been a priest for only three years and there were a good number of fellow Arab clergy who had greater experience in ministry and were more senior than I was. It seemed quite unfair to many of my colleagues, and I believe rightly so.

The work on the formation of a new church structure and constitution had to wait until the appointment of Bishop Robert Stopford. As Archbishop Appleton retired in 1974, Bishop Stopford took over as Vicar-General. He was the retired Bishop of London, an able and strong administrator. He focused his energy and talent on producing a constitution for the Central Synod of the Episcopal Church in Jerusalem and the Middle East. The Synod would be composed of four dioceses, namely, Jerusalem,[5] Iran, Cyprus and the Gulf, and Egypt and North Africa. The four dioceses would form a Province of the Anglican Communion.

Bishop Stopford was a person to be admired and respected. I watched how he formed his committees and how he worked with great love and dedication to produce a constitution not only for the new Synod but also for every one of the four dioceses. He was, indeed, an amazing person. By 1976, he completed his mandate. He was able to lay the foundation for the

5. The Jerusalem Diocese includes Jordan, Lebanon, Syria, Palestine, and Israel.

future of the Anglican Church in the Middle East. That same year, Bishop Fayeq Haddad was consecrated as the first Arab bishop in Jerusalem for the Jerusalem Diocese of the Episcopal Church in Jerusalem and the Middle East. It was a historic milestone for which many of us had advocated.

Land Day, March 30, 1976

In 1976, the Israeli government announced its decision to confiscate thousands of dunums[6] of land from its Arab (Palestinian) Israeli citizens for state purposes. This was not the first nor the last time the government of Israel would do this. But the massive areas of land slated for confiscation caused the Arab Israeli citizens, from Galilee in the north to the Negev in the south, to call for a general strike and marches to protest this grave injustice.

The Galilee area, from the inception of the state of Israel, was demographically largely Arab—both Muslim and Christian. In fact, the Christian community in Galilee was, and continues to be, quite large. To offset this, Israel continued to monitor what it regarded as a "demographic problem" and used the confiscation of Israeli Arab land and the building of new Jewish settlements as a means to alleviate this perceived threat. Due to the higher birth rate among the Arab citizens of Israel, the number of Arabs in Galilee continues to be on the rise to this day.

Several days before March 30, I was approached by the Haifa local organizing committee. They wanted to know whether they could use the St. Luke's small open playground for their venue to hold a rally to protest the Israeli government decision to confiscate Arab Israeli land. The program was to include multiple speeches condemning the government's action.

I was in full sympathy with the objective of this rally. I checked with the pastorate committee (vestry) of the church. They were also in line with the Haifa community that was going to raise its voice against the abhorrent injustice.

When the local organizers assured me of the nonviolent nature of the rally, I gave my permission. However, when the publicity leaflets were circulated all over town and the venue was going to be St. Luke's church's playground, the pressure started mounting against me to withdraw my consent. In fact, one of the local parish priests came to see me and pleaded with me to cancel the rally. He argued that this was a political event and we as a church should not be involved. He also said that if I went ahead, I would

6. Four dunums is equal to one acre.

jeopardize my ministry in Haifa. Another person got in touch to warn me that the police would not look favorably on my involvement.

On March 30, the rally took place at St. Luke's playground. Several hundred people, mainly Arab Israelis and a few Jews, attended. Multiple speakers gave their speeches, basically condemning the unjust action of the government.

Early evening of that day, Maha and I had to go to Nazareth to offer our condolences to a bereaved family. I told my mother, who was living on the first floor, that we would not be late. We took our seven-month-old Stefan with us and went on a quick run to Nazareth (about forty kilometers or twenty-four miles). When we returned, we found our front door forced open and our house broken into. Glassware was smashed and one of the speakers for the record player was stolen. The only thing of sentimental value that I regretted losing was my college ring. Other than that, nothing of value was missing. I called the police and informed them about the robbery, but they did not show up until the next morning. They did their inspection, wrote their findings, and filed their report. I never heard from them again.

One of the neighbors, whom I always suspected of collaborating with the police, dropped by to see me. He told me that what happened to my house the night before was all fabricated. The motive was not to steal. The intention was to teach me a lesson not to do it again.

That morning we heard the news that the Israeli army and police had confronted the Arab Israeli marchers in the various towns where the rallies took place, and killed six Israeli Arabs, wounded a hundred persons, and arrested another hundred. The date, March 30, 1976, continues to be commemorated each year as Land Day.

My Mother's Death

A few months later, my mother was diagnosed with colon cancer and had to undergo a colectomy. Her condition started gradually worsening until we were not able to care for her at home. We were thankful to Ebenezer Home in Haifa that kindly cared for her. After eleven days, mother went to be with the Lord. Before she died, she was happily aware that Maha and I were expecting our second child. On January 17, 1977, the funeral took place at St. John the Evangelist Episcopal Church in Haifa. She was laid to rest, however, next to my father at the church cemetery in Nazareth. She was seventy-two years old.

I give thanks to God for my mother's strong faith and trust in the Lord. She endured many difficulties with patience, serenity, and fortitude, especially when we lost our comfortable life in Beisan and became refugees in Nazareth. Throughout it all, she gave us her love and sacrificed much to meet our needs. She maintained and sustained her love of Christ to the very end. She was not only my beloved mother; I depended much on her wisdom and advice. May she and father rest in peace and rise in glory.

An Expanded Ministry

With the transfer of Assis Bayouk from Kufur Yasif to serve Emmanuel Episcopal Church in Ramleh, I was asked to look after Our Savior Episcopal Church in Akka (Acre) in addition to my ministry in Haifa. I served the church in Akka from 1977 to 1979.

With the exception of sporadic services, this church was practically closed after the Nakba of 1948. Most of the members moved away. Some went to live in Kufur Yasif. I used to celebrate the Holy Communion service once a month, first at the church building and later at the family home of Dr. Ardekian. I maintained this schedule until the end of 1979.

Political Changes and the Need for Graduate Study

In 1977, and for the first time since the inception of the state of Israel in 1948, the Likud, the right wing religious Zionist party, won the Israeli election in a landslide victory, and Menachem Begin became prime minister. It was a major turning point in the political history of Israel. Gradually, Likud became Israel's dominant party.

In the war of 1967, Israel had expanded its territory by occupying all the West Bank including East Jerusalem and the Gaza Strip. Up to that point, the Labor Party had been the dominant party in Israel, and it was relatively easy for it to form successive coalition governments. The Zionist founders of the party and the government were predominantly Labor. Most of them were secular Zionists and ideological socialists. There were two main rationales that the Israeli government and Jewish people, in general, presented in their defense for the creation and establishment of the state of Israel, namely antisemitism and the Holocaust. After the 1967 war and the

95

occupation of the West Bank including East Jerusalem (what Israel refers to as Judea and Samaria), the rationale began to shift. Instead of antisemitism and the Holocaust, it became God and the Bible. Secular Zionism, which had emphasized the evil of antisemitism that had led to the tragedy of the Holocaust, began slowly to wane and gradually was replaced by religious Zionism that emphasized God's involvement in the return of the Jews to "their" promised land. For the religious Zionists, the Bible became the "title deed" that supported Israeli a priori right to the land of Palestine.

Whereas it was easier to negotiate with the secular Zionists, it became more difficult to argue with the religious Zionists whose basic tenet was that the whole land was given exclusively to the Jewish people, and that they had the biblical documentation to prove it.

It was these drastic political changes that made me rethink the priorities of my ministry. When religious ideology started to override the political, I felt that the struggle over Palestine was not going to be resolved soon. The government of Israel would become more intransigent. It was bad enough when the secular Zionists were in power. But now, with the religious Zionists taking over, the political situation had become much worse, and our chances for achieving a just peace had become slimmer and grimmer by the day. We were now up against religious fanatics who were supported by Western Christian Zionists who were equally zealous. Both believed that the Jewish people had a "divine right" to all the land of Palestine, and they had no qualms about killing or expelling Palestinians in the name of "their God." If I wanted to contribute to peacemaking, which was a mandate by Christ himself, I needed to go back to school to receive more training so that I could be better equipped for a ministry that needed to focus on justice and peace, not only from a political perspective but, even more, from a biblical and theological perspective.

What confirmed my need for further study was the experience I acquired as a member of the Consultation on the Church and the Jewish People (CCJP) of the World Council of Churches (WCC). The chairman was Krister Stendahl, dean of Harvard Divinity School. Throughout most of the 1970s, only two members of the Consultation were Arab (Palestinian) Israelis: Rev. Ibrahim Simaan, a Baptist pastor, and me, and both of us were serving in Haifa. The Consultation was composed of scholars from the United States, Canada, the UK, Germany, and other European countries. The main objective of the Consultation was to promote Jewish-Christian dialogue. We met at least twice a year, and we always had a few Jewish scholars with us. It was a good learning experience for Ibrahim and me. It was, however, a very difficult task. We dealt with the sin of antisemitism. We analyzed, critiqued, and condemned the way Western Christians related to Jewish people in the past, and the importance of moving together into the future with love and respect for the other.

What Ibrahim and I tried to do very often was to bring into the discussion what the government of Israel had been doing to the Palestinians. We emphasized the human rights violations that Israel perpetrated. We mentioned the confiscation of Palestinian land, the building of settlements on Palestinian land, and the treatment of Palestinian prisoners. We were hoping that in our reports there would be words that reflected the importance of biblical justice, truth, and peace.

Some of the Christian scholars with us were blindly committed to the state of Israel. They defended its actions even though it violated UN resolutions and international law. Most of the members were doctors and professors, teaching in colleges and universities. Many of them paid little attention to what Ibrahim and I were sharing with them. I felt that I did not have the academic credentials that most of them had. Some of them were academically arrogant and did not respect our living personal experience of the injustice committed by Israel. They were closed to the reality on the ground which Israel had created in its oppression of the Palestinians. It was then that I decided to go for graduate work. I felt that if I wanted to contribute to justice and peacemaking, I must become more qualified and equipped academically. I discussed this with Maha, and we started praying that God would open the way and guide our future.

One day in early 1979 I went to Jerusalem for church meetings. While there I met for the first time John and Virginia Hadsell from California. John was teaching at San Francisco Theological Seminary, and he was the director of its doctoral program. We had a good visit, and they offered me a full scholarship to work on my doctorate. I went back to Haifa and discussed it with Maha. Then I got in touch with John and Virginia and accepted their offer. All the paperwork was carried out quickly and very smoothly. I did not have enough money to pay for the plane tickets, so I used the children's savings. We left Haifa in the summer of 1979; Stefan was approaching five years old, and Sari was three. We trusted the good Lord and left to go back to Berkeley, California.

According to the curriculum, I needed two full years of coursework and then the writing of a dissertation. My original intent for the dissertation was to articulate a strategy for the Episcopal Church in Israel/Palestine that could guide its work for justice and peace. My basic question was how could a small church that is rooted in its land yet oppressed by an illegal military occupation advocate for a just peace.

My research required that I immerse myself in the historical and political background of the conflict before addressing the religious, biblical, and theological understanding of justice. Only then was I able to articulate a strategy for a nonviolent approach to the stubborn and obstinate conflict. As a Christian, I believed that it was mandatory for the church to follow Jesus, its liberator, in naming and exposing the injustice and in taking a prophetic stance against the evil of oppression as well as to work for peace and reconciliation. In this dissertation, I felt guided and driven by the spirit to accomplish this task.

During our stay in Berkeley, Stefan and Sari went to school. Stefan went to first grade and Sari to kindergarten. For relaxation, I used to take the boys to the campus of the University of California at Berkeley, which was very close to where we lived. We used to run and play on the lawns. In spite of the hard study, our family spent very enjoyable times visiting different places in the Bay Area including San Francisco where Abla Aranki, Maha's sister, lived.

On our way back home, we stopped in Texas to visit our relatives. I was invited to fill in at St. Luke's Episcopal Church in Dallas for two months, and then returned to Haifa to resume my parish ministry at St. John the Evangelist Episcopal Church.

Part III

The Intifada[7] and the Birth of Palestinian Liberation Theology

7. The Intifada was the "uprising" of the Palestinian people against the illegal Israeli occupation. The word 'intifada' is Arabic for "shaking off."

9

Going Up to Jerusalem

The Intifada

THE 1980s SAW A rise in Palestinian frustration with the military occupation and its accompanying checkpoints, arbitrary arrests, home demolitions, and other human rights abuses. For me, it would be a time when I would strive to support an increasing nonviolent resistance to occupation while navigating church politics and raising a family with Maha.

In 1982, while we were still in Berkeley, the church council (Majma) elected Archdeacon Samir Kafity as coadjutor bishop. It was after midnight when our phone in our Berkeley apartment rang. It was Archdeacon Kafity informing us that he had been elected. In January 1984, he became the second Arab Anglican bishop in Jerusalem after the retirement of Bishop Fayeq Haddad.

I returned to Jerusalem to attend Bishop Kafity's investiture service at St. George's Cathedral on January 6, 1984. It was a great occasion with the presence of many local and international guests, in addition to many church members from around the diocese. The Shefa Amer and Haifa choirs joined together, and we went up to Jerusalem to lead the singing at the service. We sang the hymns the bishop had chosen, and the cathedral vibrated with the beautiful sound of the singers.

Several months later, Bishop Kafity indicated that he would like to appoint me as the general executive secretary of the diocese and Majma, as well as the pastor of the Palestinian Arab congregation at St. George's Cathedral where he was serving. I tried to persuade the bishop to appoint someone else. In fact, I mentioned the name of another fellow priest whom I thought would be more suitable to the position. The bishop kept insisting that I was the person he wanted. I liked Bishop Kafity and respected him. In addition to being a charismatic and gifted leader, he was an eloquent speaker and a good preacher. He had an outgoing personality and was liked by many people. His style was Arabic oratory, and his use of the Arabic language was very good. Maha knew him long before I did, when he was still a deacon in Ramallah and Birzeit, and later when he was serving as the minister of All Saints Church in Beirut, where she worshiped regularly while she was studying at Beirut University College (BUC). His home was always open to university students and friends. I only met him when he returned to Jerusalem. We became friends and colleagues, and I wanted to maintain my friendship with him. I feared that working very closely with him might stir up certain difficulties that could spoil the friendship and I really wanted to avoid that.

When I was trying to persuade the bishop to appoint someone else, I was conscious of my own vulnerabilities and weak points. I knew that God had given me an independent and free spirit, and if I disliked or disagreed with the bishop's decisions, I would not be able to go along with him or support him. I could not be a "yes sir" person. It was this knowledge of my inner makeup that caused me to hesitate in accepting the new position the bishop offered me. But he insisted, and, in the end, I accepted, but deep within me I was apprehensive.

General Executive Secretary

In January 1985, our family left Haifa for Jerusalem. In my capacity as executive secretary, I tried to apply the regulations of the church council to upgrade the administrative and pastoral ministry in the diocese. We were able to renovate the office space, furnish it adequately, and employ multiple staff, men and women, for the various tasks needed, including a professional accountant for the diocese. The bishop approved all the appointments and the office started to run as smoothly as expected.

One of the innovative ideas I introduced was a weekly Holy Communion service for the staff in one of the small chapels at the Cathedral. I felt deeply that our meetings for prayer and communion would not only revitalize us but would keep Christ at the center of our work. None of the staff objected, although they belonged to various church denominations in the city. Before long, I felt that the weekly Eucharist kept us spiritually energized and job-focused.

The first year as executive secretary went well. The bishop and I would frequently consult with one another on various issues. I was pleased that he trusted me, and we coordinated things together. I tried to introduce some changes in the elections of pastorate committees (vestries) and he supported the changes. I also tried to introduce a new concept for the annual meeting of the Majma. Instead of the church delegates coming to hear only reports and discuss the financial statement, I felt that it was important to stimulate their thinking by having time for discussion on crucial and relevant issues that faced and challenged the church. I felt there was a great need for our church's leadership to be abreast of what was going on locally and internationally. Some people did not appreciate the change. They were in a hurry to return home and resisted the proposed new format.

The Jerusalem Parish

I was able to organize my pastoral ministry in the Palestinian congregation at the cathedral. We formed a small group of three members of the pastorate committee (vestry) to accompany me every Tuesday evening to visit two church families each week. This was welcomed and appreciated because many of the families enjoyed a pastoral visit.

I started a choir, but soon realized that our church members did not have the quality voices I was looking for. Nevertheless, I focused on teaching them new hymns and then through them, we taught the congregation on Sundays. Living under occupation in East Jerusalem was difficult for St. George's Palestinian congregation. Slowly Israel was restricting the movement of people from the northern suburbs to East Jerusalem. Despite that, some faithful people did their best to come to the 9:30 morning worship service. It was not easy, but I was able to maintain contact with the church family through pastoral care and regular parish visits. Slowly church attendance began to increase. It became noticeable that a good number of children began to come to Sunday school and a healthy church atmosphere began to form.

On Sunday morning at St. George's Cathedral, we had two services, the 9:30 worship service in Arabic and the 11:00 service in English. On all feast days, the bishop was the preacher. On most other Sundays, I would preach, which I always enjoyed. When I started my ministry at the cathedral, church attendance was composed mainly of the Palestinian congregation. Gradually, especially after the Intifada, an increasing number of expatriates started coming to worship with us. This trend began to increase. Toward the end of my ministry, the number of visitors overwhelmed the Palestinian congregation. I had to resort to a bilingual service every Sunday, especially when the United Methodist Church in the States encouraged its members to spend time with the local indigenous Christians of the land. On some Sundays, our attendance would swell to almost two hundred people.

It was during my second year as executive secretary of the diocese that I started feeling a change in the bishop's attitude toward me. Slowly I felt excluded from some meetings. Decisions that should have involved me were made without my knowledge. Instead of the previous direct communication between us, it became indirect. I shared my frustration with Maha, and I began to fear the consequences. In diocesan matters where I should have been involved, some clergy started bypassing me by going directly to the bishop while I remained in the dark. Such tactics affected my work and my diocesan staff felt it.

I cannot put all the blame on the bishop, because I started to react to the bishop's behavior, and I became part of the problem. I did not appreciate the two-faced approach and I confronted the bishop multiple times. He did not level with me. It was difficult for me to pretend that things were okay. I always went to him prepared with points and examples, but it was clear that we were moving apart rather than toward each other.

Things got worse and rather than have him fire me, I eventually took the initiative and resigned from my job as executive secretary. This act must have angered him a lot. Since I had the dual responsibility of being both the secretary of the diocese and Majma as well as the pastor of the congregation, I expected that I would be assigned the pastorate of another church and would have to move out of Jerusalem. This fact concerned me most due to our children's schooling. I wished I had never left Haifa.

As it turned out, some of the prominent members of the parish met with the bishop on their own and asked him to leave me in Jerusalem as the pastor of the congregation and find someone else to take over the administrative work of the executive secretary of the diocese. To the bishop's credit, he allowed me to stay in Jerusalem as pastor, but unfortunately, our relationship was never the same after that.

With hindsight, and in spite of the pain it caused me, everything turned out for the best for the next phase of my ministry.

An Important Turning Point

In the spring of 1987, a few months before the outbreak of the first intifada, Marc Ellis came to visit Jerusalem with his wife and baby, Aaron. A few months before, his book *Toward a Jewish Theology of Liberation* had been published by Orbis Books. Marc was invited to speak on his new book at the Shalom Hartman Institute in West Jerusalem. Two respondents were chosen: Michael Walzer, an American Jewish professor from Princeton, and Father Elias Chacour, a Palestinian Israeli Melkite priest from Galilee.

A few days before this event, Kathy Bergen came to see me at St. George's Anglican/Episcopal Cathedral in East Jerusalem. Kathy was a Mennonite missionary activist working among the Palestinians. I was the canon pastor of the Palestinian congregation at the Cathedral. Kathy informed me that Marc Ellis, an American Jewish theologian, would be visiting Jerusalem to introduce his new book and asked if I would be interested in being a respondent.

I told Kathy that I was tired of listening to American scholars who come to pontificate and tell us what we need to do as Palestinians, but do not have courage to speak prophetically against the injustice perpetrated by the government of Israel. So, I declined, but before the event took place, Kathy got in touch again and encouraged me to attend. When we arrived, the place was packed, mostly with young people. As far as I could tell, Fr. Elias Chacour and I were the only Palestinians present.

I was impressed with Marc's courage and articulate presentation. I could tell that he was nervous and that he was speaking to an unfriendly and skeptical audience. I don't remember the contents of his message nor the points that the two respondents gave, but I remember the electric atmosphere in the hall. Marc spoke with candor and truthfulness, and I could feel that people were uneasy with his input and approach. Michael Walzer was critical, mean, and condescending. It bothered me to feel the level of hostility against Marc that bordered on ridicule. Fr. Chacour was supportive and appreciative of Marc. It seemed that Fr. Chacour, Kathy, and I were the only ones on Marc's side. Although I had not met Marc, I felt proud of him and at the same time sorry for the way he was being received and treated.

During the discussion afterward, most of those who spoke blamed the Palestinians for the conflict and defended Israel's actions. Marc tried to reach out to them and challenge their assumptions, mistruths, and lack of personal introspections. It was a very tense evening, but I was glad to have been there and to have met Marc. Despite the intense opposition, Marc stood his ground and communicated his message.

After the event, I invited Marc and his family to our apartment at the cathedral for dinner the next day. We had a good evening together. He gave me a copy of his book, *Toward a Jewish Theology of Liberation*, and I handed him a packet of a manuscript of my doctoral dissertation that I was hoping to publish into a book. He offered to take it back with him to Maryknoll and present it to Orbis Books for publication.

The dissertation covered the historical, political, and religious background of the Palestine-Israel conflict. It also included a Palestinian Christian theology of justice since the main cause of the conflict has been the injustice, dispossession, expulsion, and continued occupation and oppression brought about by Jewish Zionists against our Palestinian people. The gist of the dissertation included a theology of the God of justice, righteousness, truth, mercy, peace, and reconciliation. It addressed the dilemmas of power and law vis-à-vis justice and emphasized the prophetic and peacemaking imperative of the church in the resolution of the conflict.

The Intifada Erupts

Several months later, the first intifada erupted, and it changed and revolutionized my subsequent ministry.

The spark that lit the flame of the intifada started on December 8, 1987, when an Israeli Jewish driver drove his semi-trailer into two Palestinian cars in Gaza, killing four Palestinians and injuring seven. The pot of violence had been simmering for a long time. The Israeli army was killing and imprisoning Palestinians frequently. The Palestinians could not forget Israel's invasion of Lebanon and the killing of over nineteen thousand people, many of them Palestinians, including the massacres in the Sabra and Shatila refugee camps. Eventually, the pot boiled over, and their patience could not take it any longer. The Palestinians were waiting for the United Nations to implement its own resolutions and rescue them from the oppressive yoke of the Israeli occupation. Tragically, the international community was too weak and incapable of bringing liberation. The intifada reflected the nonviolent uprising of an oppressed people. The Israeli government could not crush it.

Statement by Patriarchs and Bishops

Seeing the intifada gaining momentum and vigor by early 1988. I discussed the matter with Bishop Kafity. I argued that as the intifada was gaining strength and popularity throughout the Palestinian community from Gaza to Jerusalem and the West Bank, and it was clearly nonviolent in its thrust, it was essential that the heads of the Christian churches express their solidarity and support for the uprising.

In those days there was no official presence of the PLO (Palestine Liberation Organization) in Palestine. The PLO leadership was in exile in Tunis.[1] Be that as it may, we had multiple good local political leaders, Muslims and Christians, such as Faisal Husseini, Hanan Ashrawi, and others. Bishop Kafity approved the idea and gave me permission to work out the details. We agreed that I should contact all the patriarchs and bishops, beginning with the Orthodox patriarch since he is considered the bishop (patriarch) of Jerusalem. I worked on a draft and personally handed it to Bishop Timothy, the Orthodox patriarch's representative. Then I visited the Latin patriarch, Michel Sabbah, who had been recently appointed by the Vatican as the first Arab Latin patriarch in Jerusalem. I did the same with the Armenian patriarch.

We worked together on the editing and once the Orthodox and the Latins approved it, the other bishops accepted it. I worked late into the night, sending the statement to the Vatican, World Council of Churches, Middle East Council of Churches, and the National Council of Churches in New York. It was sent on January 22, 1988.[2] To my knowledge, it was the first statement that was signed by the heads of the churches in Jerusalem regarding the worsening political situation in Palestine.

Bishop Timothy got in touch with me early the following morning to tell me that he had been berated by a high official from Israel's foreign ministry, who could not believe that the heads of the churches could dare write such a statement.

1. The Unified Leadership of the Uprising was in regular contact (by fax!) with the PLO in Tunis, with both sides discussing possible strategies for resistance. Excellent summaries of the intifada can be obtained from al Haq, or the *Journal of Palestine Studies*.

2. A copy can be found in May, *Jerusalem Testament*, 13–14.

What was significant for me was that the statement broke the ice. The church truly dared to speak truth to power. It was a prophetic statement that did not mince words. It addressed the thoughts and feelings of the Christian community of the land and called for the end of Israel's occupation of the Palestinian territories.

Theological Reflection on the Intifada

When it became clear that the intifada was taking hold throughout occupied Palestine from the Gaza Strip to Jerusalem and to all the West Bank, I started inviting the worshipping congregation at St. George's every Sunday to stay after coffee to reflect on my sermons that purposefully addressed our response as Christians to the intifada and its ramifications. We reflected on questions such as, "What is our responsibility as Christians in resisting the occupation of our country?" "What should be our response as Christians in confronting injustice and oppression?" "How have our people's lives been affected by the intifada and where is Christ taking his stand?"

In those days, we were fortunate to have worshiping with us, on a regular basis, Dr. Kenneth Bailey who was an Arabist and a New Testament scholar. He was an American Presbyterian minister, and I considered him an older brother and one of my mentors. Occasionally, I invited him to preach in Arabic to our Palestinian congregation. As our people were passionately discussing what should be our Christian response to the intifada, I always looked to Dr. Bailey to share his thoughts and ideas from his Christian perspective.

Those discussions every Sunday after worship became a hallmark of St. George's congregational spiritual vitality. More Palestinian Christians from outside our congregation started coming to worship with us and to take part in the discussion. At times, those who could not make it to church came just for the discussion. One of those was attorney Jonathan Kuttab. People came with great enthusiasm. For many, the church suddenly became relevant. At least, it was addressing relevant issues that were vital to their everyday life. We used to begin by reflecting on the sermon. They amplified it by using examples and illustrations from the daily news they were hearing. Many of them were interpreting the gospel contextually and how this challenged their lives. It made me always wish that I could preach the sermon after the discussion rather than before.

The discussion was a therapeutic session. People brought their stories of police and army brutality the previous week. They shared their own pain as well as the pain of their neighbors and community and how it affected them. They mentioned the names of young men and women who had been beaten, injured, and arrested. Some of our young people at St. George's were arrested and taken to jail. It was a therapy session where our members were engaged in being therapists for each other.

The discussion was a prayer session. We always prayed for all those who were suffering and jailed. We prayed for justice and for our oppressed people. We prayed for the use of nonviolent resistance. We prayed for the needy families and discussed how we could be of help.

It was a teaching session. These discussions led us into talking about how we understood the meaning of the gospel and how our faith was being tested by the oppressive occupation. We looked at biblical texts and discussed them. The whole issue of suffering and pain was frequently discussed and where God stood in all this, and how we, as people of faith, could sustain our faith and trust in a loving and just God in the midst of the Israeli occupation and oppression.

It was a theological session. One of the great discoveries that revolutionized our discussion happened when many of our people focused their reflection on the humanity of Jesus. They saw him as a human being who experienced pain and suffering just like we do. They saw him as having been born under the Roman occupation and becoming a refugee as a child. They saw him as having lived all his life under a brutal Roman occupation and finally having been killed by the occupation forces. Such a discovery led us to focus on the life of Jesus. How did Jesus cope with life under occupation and how could he help us to cope and resist? Jesus became the paradigm of our faith, the center and focus of our discussion. We accepted him as our liberator, and we evaluated and measured our ideas, theology, and action in light of our faith and trust in him. He became our hermeneutic. He helped us remain grounded in the love of God and our love of neighbor. All this had direct practical implications for our standing for truth and justice, and for resisting everything that dehumanized and damaged God's good creation.

Finally, these discussions helped us not only to reflect on ourselves but also on our enemies. Some of our people were being greatly challenged by Jesus' words in Matt 5:43–45: "Love your enemies and pray for those who persecute you, so that you may be children of your Father in heaven; for he makes his sun rise on the evil and on the good, and sends rain on the righteous and on the unrighteous." At the same time, we challenged each other to rise to the higher standard of Jesus rather than to lower his standard to fit our own bigotries and prejudices.

As I mentioned before, this was taking place every Sunday when the Palestinian community of faith at St. George's Cathedral was reflecting on the meaning of its faith and Christian responsibility in the face of Israeli injustice and oppression. These Sunday discussions after church continued for a good number of years. The time came when we had to conduct the discussion in both Arabic and English as expatriates from around the world were coming to worship God with us and taking part in the discussions.

All this was happening before my first book was published and Sabeel was established. During those discussions, I was not aware that we were making history. We were laying the foundation for a movement that, by the grace of God, was soon to sprout and grow. What was happening to us at St. George's during the intifada reminded us of what happened on the Day of Pentecost when the Holy Spirit was poured out on the disciples, bringing new life and vitality to the followers of Jesus.

10

A Book Is Born amidst Hope and Trepidation

A Fruitful Invitation

ORBIS ACCEPTED THE MANUSCRIPT that Marc Ellis had sent to them in 1987 and invited me in April of 1988 to Maryknoll in upstate New York, where Orbis is situated, to finalize the editing. Orbis assigned one of their editors, Eve Drogin, to work with me. Eve was an American Jew, but she was a professional editor. Although I was skeptical of Eve to begin with, it was the best decision Orbis made for me. It was truly providential. Eve was quick to catch any sentences, paragraphs, or ideas that needed to be reworded so that I would not be misunderstood or accused of antisemitism. I was truly thankful to have her for an editor.

Since I had not anticipated the emergence of the intifada, I had no mention of it in my manuscript that Marc Ellis brought to Orbis. Furthermore, there was a need to make some important changes and additions to the manuscript. I was thankful to be there to complete the edit despite the difficulty of leaving Maha with Stefan (13), Sari (11), and Nevart (4) in Jerusalem.

I lived with the Maryknoll fathers for almost three months. They were friendly and warm. Their cumulative experience acquired from being missionaries in various countries of the world, and especially in Latin America, was simply amazing. I admired their dedication and sacrifice of spending the best years of their lives serving Christ among the poor and destitute of the world.

Maryknoll had a good library. Every day I spent my time researching and writing and then working with Eve. I was internally driven and wanted to do the best I could for the holistic message of the book.

A Title Is Revealed

While I was at Maryknoll, I was wondering about the title that I could suggest for my book. I was attracted by the words from Deut 16:20, "Justice, and only justice, you shall pursue. . . ." One day Eve called me for a meeting with the editorial board of Orbis. They informed me that the manuscript that I had written expressed a liberation theology for Palestine. After discussing this together, we agreed that the title of the book should be *Justice, and Only Justice*, with a subtitle, *A Palestinian Theology of Liberation*.[1] Importantly, when the book was published in 1989, the cover had the colors of the Palestinian flag (black, red, white, and green), as well as the blue and white colors of the Israeli flag. The implication was clear that if Israel wanted to live in peace in the land with the Palestinians, it must accomplish two "justices." If Israel believed that it had received justice in the creation of the state of Israel, its justice was partial and incomplete because it did not pursue the second justice. Without justice for the Palestinians, whatever justice Israel thinks it has acquired will never bring it peace or security. In the original Hebrew of Deut 16:20, the text reads, "Justice, justice you shall pursue." If the first justice meant justice for Jews after their Holocaust, the second justice must be for the Palestinians after their Nakba. Unless the Palestinians receive their justice, the first justice for Israel will continue to be shaky and precarious. In order for all the people of the land of Palestine and Israel to live in safety and security, Israel must do justice to the Palestinians by allowing them to establish their own sovereign state in accordance with the demands of international law and UN resolutions. This is the only justice that can make the resulting peace prevail and endure.

I will always be thankful to Marc Ellis for introducing me to Orbis and for all his help. Our meeting in Jerusalem in the spring of 1987 was the beginning of a life-long friendship. I consider Marc as one of the most courageous Jewish prophetic voices of our time. It is important to note that in

1. Ateek, *Justice*.

2018, a few friends of Marc organized a Festschrift in his honor at Southern Methodist University (SMU) in Dallas, Texas. It was a privilege to take part in this celebration.[2]

After leaving Maryknoll, having completed the manuscript for publication, and on my way back to Jerusalem, I attended the Lambeth Conference[3] that was taking place at the University of Kent in Canterbury between July 16 and August 3, 1988. Usually, bishops and spouses attend the Lambeth Conference. I was invited with two other priests from the Anglican Peace and Justice Network to present and discuss a special report of the network. Over five hundred Anglican bishops attended the conference from around the world. The general theme was "The Truth Shall Make You Free." Several reports were presented and there were important discussions on the topic of "Christ and people of other faiths." One of the major decisions taken was that each province respect the decisions of other provinces in the ordination and consecration of women to the episcopate.

A Serendipitous Encounter

One of the invited speakers to Lambeth 1988 was Gustavo Gutierrez, the father of Latin American liberation theology. I had met Gustavo at Maryknoll a few months before when we had a chance to spend some time together. We shared with one another the situation in Latin America and the impact of liberation theology, and I shared with him the situation in Palestine/Israel. He showed great interest in the Palestinian people and their struggle for justice as I related to him the political and economic situation under the oppressive occupation of the Israeli government. I also shared with him the abuse of the Bible by Christian Zionists and the great need to address this theological menace. I felt a close affinity to Gustavo and quickly a bond of friendship developed between us.

When I saw on the Lambeth program that he was scheduled to speak to the Anglican bishops, I sought him out, and we had the opportunity to spend more time together. In one of our discussions, he mentioned the opposition to liberation theology by Cardinal Joseph Ratzinger (later Pope

2. The book was published in 2021 by Rowman & Littlefield under the title *The New Diaspora and the Global Prophetic*, by Scholz and Slabodsky.

3. The Lambeth Conference is a gathering of bishops from around the Anglican Communion who are invited by the Archbishop of Canterbury approximately every ten years at Canterbury. The first Lambeth conference was held in 1867.

Benedict) who was the prefect of the congregation for doctrine of the faith. Ratzinger believed that liberation theology was a threat to the faith of the church, and he resisted it, and Latin American liberation theologians were unsettled and anxious about what the cardinal could do to them. Gustavo was concerned and uneasy that Ratzinger might find out about his presentation at Lambeth. Gustavo was well received by the Anglican bishops from around the world, and he gave a strong and wonderful presentation about liberation theology in Latin America and "God's preferential option for the poor."[4]

Years later, in May 2015, Pope Francis invited Gustavo Gutierrez to the Vatican as an honored guest and speaker at an event. All previous anxieties and apprehension about liberation theology had dissipated.

After Lambeth 1988, I returned to Jerusalem and resumed my parish ministry at St. George's Cathedral with the Palestinian congregation.

The Publication of *Justice, and Only Justice*

In June 1989, I received the first printing of *Justice, and Only Justice: A Palestinian Theology of Liberation*. It contained two major surprises. The first was the fact that Dr. Rosemary Radford Ruether wrote the foreword. Reading the foreword recently, I was amazed at its relevance to the conflict after over thirty years since its writing. In one of its paragraphs, Rosemary wrote, "This land of three faiths cursed by its 'holiness' can become a land of blessing only when it becomes clear to all three that it is a land that cannot be claimed by one people only. It is a land of two peoples, Israeli Jews and Palestinians. It is a land of three faiths, Judaism, Christianity, and Islam. The key to peace is the acknowledgment that this land must be shared. The path to blessing is to learn how to share it."[5]

The second surprise was the endorsements of three well-known scholars that appeared on the back cover, namely, Dr. John H. Yoder, Dr. Dale Bishop, and Dr. Marc H. Ellis. John Yoder wrote, "Naim Ateek provides an authentic restatement of the gospel message of liberation within the very special setting of the Palestinian tragedy." Dale Bishop wrote, "Ateek's work is . . . an engaging attempt to articulate an authentic Middle Eastern theology of liberation, one that has as its focus the Palestinian people." For Marc

---

4. God's preferential option for the poor is the central tenet of Gutierrez, *Theology of Liberation*.

5. Ateek, *Justice*, xii.

Ellis, the book "represents a challenge to integrate Palestinian voices into our own [Jewish] theology and thus help create a path of solidarity where distrust and fear abound."

In the fall of 1989, *Justice, and Only Justice: A Palestinian Theology of Liberation* was launched at St. George's McInnes Hall under the patronage of Bishop Samir Kafity. In spite of my shaky relationship with the bishop, he was kind and supportive of my book. I had expressed my gratitude to him in the acknowledgment section of the book. He gave a very good and thoughtful introductory word.

I was thankful that the book was received well and with a good measure of excitement by the Christian and Muslim community of Jerusalem. Looking back, the publication of the book marked the beginning of a non-violent movement based clearly and consciously on the strong foundation of our Christian understanding of the love of God and love of neighbor. We hoped that a movement would grow by the grace and power of God to witness and advocate for a just peace for the Palestinian people and for all the people of our land.

11

Historic Visits in the Midst of the Intifada

IN THE EARLY YEARS of the intifada, we were blessed with the visits of two giants who came and supported Palestinian resistance: Nobel Laureate and the Archbishop of Cape Town, Desmond Tutu, and the former US President Jimmy Carter.

Archbishop Desmond Tutu Electrifies Jerusalem

In December 1989, at the invitation of Bishop Samir Kafity, Archbishop Desmond Tutu came to visit the Holy Land around Christmas time. I had the privilege of meeting the archbishop the year before during the Lambeth Conference in England in 1988. In fact, we were paired together in one of the Lambeth committees and ended up spending time together drafting one of the Lambeth documents. This happened one year before my first book was published, and seven months after the start of the first intifada in December 1987. When I met Archbishop Tutu in Lambeth, I shared with him the spiritual awakening that had been taking place at St. George's Cathedral when the Palestinian Anglican/Episcopal congregation was meeting every Sunday after the morning Eucharist to discuss what it means to be a Christian living under occupation.

Long before Archbishop Tutu came to visit Jerusalem, we were aware that he stood with our Palestinian people against the injustice of the Israeli government with the same courage he displayed in speaking out against apartheid in South Africa.

Archbishop Tutu arrived in Jerusalem on the afternoon of December 22, 1989. His first engagement was to preach at the Christmas Eve service of readings and carols at Shepherds' Field in Beit Sahour. When we approached Beit Sahour, I could not believe my eyes. Thousands of people, Christians and Muslims, had swarmed the Shepherds' Field. There was no room for us to go through the crowd to reach the cave at the end of the YMCA property. When we reached the place, the Israeli army was stationed outside the fence with their full military gear. We started the service with Bishop Kafity presiding. I was playing the small organ accompanied by Stefan and Sari on their trumpet and trombone. The sound of the Christmas carols reverberated as people sang, "Hark! the herald angels sing, 'Glory to the newborn king.'" Men and women took turns reading the Christmas story with carols interspersed in between the readings. When the time came for Archbishop Tutu to speak, he would tell stories about oppressed people, about police and army brutality, then pause and say, "I am only speaking about South Africa," and the Palestinian crowd would roar with laughter, because everything he said applied to the situation in Palestine. He would then continue with another story and pause and say, "I am only speaking about South Africa." Using this style, he communicated a strong message about the injustice and oppression our people were subjected to under the illegal Israeli occupation. The archbishop talked about the birth of Jesus and concluded with a prophetic message of hope that God is a God of justice and that the injustice would eventually end and the Palestinians would achieve liberation and peace.

That evening, the Christmas service of carols at the Church of the Nativity in Bethlehem was followed by the Christmas Holy Communion service at St. George's Cathedral in Jerusalem. As Bishop Kafity was reading the consecration prayer with the clergy and Archbishop Tutu around him, a person came and handed me a note that said that there was a bomb inside the cathedral. When I relayed the message to Bishop Kafity, he suggested that we needed to exit the cathedral. Without disclosing the note, I asked the congregation to start singing another carol while moving out quietly to the cathedral courtyard. In the courtyard, people formed a large circle and, as we served them communion, they innocently sang Christmas carols a cappella. Although it was late December, it was not raining, and the weather was cold but pleasant. The police searched the cathedral and found nothing. It was just a bomb scare that was intended to disrupt the service where the archbishop was preaching. After communion was served, we offered our thanksgiving prayer, sang a final carol, and Bishop Kafity gave us the Christmas blessing and we were dismissed. The following morning a graffiti painted on the wall outside St. George's Cathedral read, "Tutu, a black, Nazi pig."

I had the privilege of accompanying Bishop Kafity and Archbishop Tutu in their visits to the Israeli Ministry of Religion. I was impressed by his prophetic words as he candidly spoke about the need for justice and liberation for the Palestinian people. Archbishop Tutu's short five-day visit had a positive impact on all of us.

Several years later, with the help of Bishop Browning, the presiding bishop of the Episcopal Church in the United States, Archbishop Desmond Tutu became the international patron of Sabeel. His commitment to justice for the Palestinians never wavered.

Archbishop Tutu was the main speaker at two major Friends of Sabeel events in Old South Church, Boston. His presence attracted a thousand people. In his first visit there was a pro-Israel and Christian Zionist crowd with banners and signs picketing the Sabeel event, but the police stood guard and the occasion passed by peacefully.

One week after Archbishop Tutu's visit, the leadership of the intifada organized a chain of people, men and women, locals and expatriates, holding hands and encircling the Old City of Jerusalem. I felt proud of our Palestinian people who were resisting the occupation of Jerusalem and the Palestinian territories in a nonviolent way. I participated with some friends but later that afternoon, the Israeli military came and sprayed us with colored water and broke the chain. But it did not change our determination to continue nonviolent resistance.

The President of the United States

In March 1990, former President Jimmy Carter came to visit Jerusalem. During that time, I was active in the United Christian Council in Israel (UCCI), which was made up of largely Protestant Christians—expatriate clergy and laypeople and a few local Christian clergy and laity who shared concerns about the injustice of the occupation. The greatest concern of the expatriate evangelicals, especially the American pastors, was the anti-missionary legislation that the Knesset had enacted in order to appease the Israeli religious parties.

The American Southern Baptist pastors arranged a meeting with President Carter late at night. I was invited to join them largely because I was, at that time, the president of the UCCI. The president welcomed us at his suite at the Jerusalem Hilton Hotel. I presented him with a copy of my book, *Justice, and Only Justice*, and shared our concerns about the occupation of our land and the injustice and oppression of our people. My Baptist friends shared their concern about the anti-missionary law that the Israeli Knesset had legislated. We had a good but brief discussion with him. Throughout, he was gracious and kind. I often wondered whether he had read my book and whether I contributed in a small way to the biblical and theological perspective of justice and peace from a Palestinian viewpoint.

Years later I had the privilege of meeting President Carter a few more times, including my visit to the Carter Center in Atlanta, Georgia. During his presidency, his Christian faith impacted his governance. Despite being a one-term president, he was able to broker a peace treaty between Egypt and Israel, which led to the withdrawal of Israel from the Sinai and its return to Egypt. One thing for sure, he continued to promote justice and peace for the Palestinians. The epitome of this was in the publication of his book, *Palestine: Peace Not Apartheid*.[1] The title of the book said it all. The president had come to the conclusion that, after he had invested so much time in working for peace, the Israeli leadership's policies toward the Palestinians were closer to apartheid than peace. President Carter understood that peace and making peace is at the heart of being an authentic human being, and, from a Christian perspective, being a child of God as Jesus said in the Beatitudes (Matt 5:9). President Carter tried, but Israel was not ready for a peace based on justice. I often wonder what he might have accomplished for Palestinian and Israeli justice had he been elected to a second term.

Yet more years later, in August of 2009, Tutu and Carter visited Palestine together. Two media quotes from their visit are worth sharing. From Jimmy Carter: "Although it's very important now to stop all the settlement building and expansion in all of Palestine, including East Jerusalem, that's just a first step. The final step will have to be for all Israeli settlements to be removed from Palestine. And let there be an independent nation here on

---

1. Carter, *Palestine*.

this land where we're standing side by side in peace with Israel being the ultimate goal."[2]

And from Desmond Tutu: "You don't get true security from the barrel of a gun. They tried to oppress us with the barrel of a gun. They found that, in the end, true security came when the human rights of all were recognized and respected."[3]

2. "Carter: All Israeli Settlements."
3. "Carter: All Israeli Settlements."

Part IV

Sabeel

12

The Birth of a Movement

IN 1990, WITH THE publication of *Justice, and Only Justice*, Palestinian liberation theology had emerged as a theological response to the conflict. Fr. Tom Stransky, director of Tantur Ecumenical Institute in Jerusalem, approached me to give lectures on Palestinian liberation theology (PLT) to Notre Dame students as well as to their continuing education program for clergy. I found it very satisfying and an important vehicle to share PLT and the struggle for justice and peace. In the same year (1990), we held an international conference at Tantur in order to introduce my book to a wider segment of the Palestinian Christian community in the Jerusalem area. This took place before the Sabeel Center came into being and before Orbis Books published our first book, *Faith and the Intifada*.

Understanding the Political Changes

The 1990s had arrived with the continuation of the intifada, which had begun at the end of 1987. For six years, the intifada and the resistance continued. It came to a halt with the Oslo agreement in 1993 that recognized the PLO as the sole representative of the Palestinian people, and most of the Palestinians celebrated the return of the PLO leadership to Ramallah and the West Bank. Indeed, with mixed feelings of joy and apprehension, we all enjoyed seeing the Palestinian flag flying high in the Jerusalem sky. I still remember watching, from the balcony of our apartment, the great rally that took place at St. George's School football field with a few thousand Palestinians celebrating and raising hundreds of Palestinian flags in East Jerusalem, an action that had until then been considered illegal. Unfortunately, instead of the end of the occupation and the birthing of liberation, Oslo turned out to be a deceptive political formula that brought greater disaster on our people.

The Oslo agreements had many shortcomings for the Palestinian side. One of the main shortcomings was to avoid dealing with the major issues—defining the borders, the issue of the illegal Jewish settlements in the West Bank, Jerusalem, the Palestinian refugees—and pushing them to the final stage, supposedly to build trust between the sides. In hindsight, it was a trap. The Israelis cheated the Palestinians into believing that Oslo would lead to the establishment of an independent Palestinian State by 1999. However, on September 28, 2000, the then Israeli Minister of Defense, Ariel Sharon, provocatively entered the Al Aqsa Mosque compound, accompanied with around one thousand Israeli soldiers. This act triggered the second intifada, which turned into violence and bloodshed.

It was during the decade of the '90s, during all these historic events, that Sabeel took root.

Beginnings

In the earliest stage of the Palestinian liberation theology movement, as I was still discerning the will of God for the next possible stage, I invited a few trusted friends to help me think through the decisions that needed to be taken. These friends became the founding members of Sabeel—Samia Khoury, Cedar Duaybis, Jean Zaru, Jonathan Kuttab, Father (later Bishop) Elias Chacour, and Assis (later Bishop) Riah Abu El Assal.[1] I give thanks to God for these founders of Sabeel who for many years also served as its first board. Jean became vice president, Samia was our treasurer, and Cedar served as secretary.

---

1. These friends were already active advocates for Palestinian justice and against the Israeli occupation. Samia was active with the YWCA and was the head of the board at Rawdat el-Zuhur; Cedar became very active with Sabeel (see later); Jean served on the central committee with the World Council of Churches; Jonathan, as an attorney, was active politically and religiously; Fr. Chacour had written *Blood Brothers* and was known internationally as an advocate for peace and justice, and later Abu El Assal wrote *Caught in Between* and was very active politically with the Democratic Front.

In the absence of a proper name for the nascent movement, we referred to ourselves as "the PLT Group." In those days, the word "liberation" was novel and problematic. In Arabic, it was only used in a political sense by the PLO (Palestine Liberation Organization), and none of us gave it a theological connotation. One of our first tasks was to help people make sense of the connection between liberation and theology.

On Friday, January 22, 1993, the PLT Group adopted the name Sabeel for the movement. We had a committee meeting in Tiberias at the Scottish Hospice (now Scots Hotel) to make it easier for our members from the north to attend. Some of us were not sure where our nascent "movement" was going. I was praying for guidance to discern whether we should grow the movement.

On the way to Tiberias, we started suggesting possible names for this novel theology. Some of the names had been already taken by other political and social organizations, but we kept brainstorming. I believe it was Cedar who first suggested the word "Sabeel." Sabeel is Arabic for "the way," and it also means a spring of fresh and life-giving water. We all felt the appropriateness of the name, not only for the suitability of its meaning, but also the ease of its pronunciation for our expatriate friends. I confess that although I immediately liked the name, I did not fully comprehend the depth and relevance of its historical and spiritual connotation. It later dawned on me that we had stumbled on, or more correctly, providentially been guided to, a significant discovery. It was in Jerusalem that the early followers of Jesus Christ were referred to as the people of the "Way" (Acts 9:2; 19:9, 23; 24:14, 22). And now, two thousand years later, a new small community in Jerusalem was choosing the name Sabeel to walk the way in the footsteps of Jesus Christ who said, "I am the way, the truth, and the life" (John 14:6), the way of love and compassion, justice and truth, peace and reconciliation. Sabeel is an active word that describes a movement of people around the world who are committed to the liberation of the Palestinian people.

There is another significant dimension of the word Sabeel. It is not only an Arabic word that is used only by Christians; it is a word that is familiar to Muslims and Jews. It is mentioned in both the Quran and the Torah, carrying the same meaning of the way and path.

So, it was in that meeting in Tiberias on the shores of the Sea of Galilee that the name Sabeel was adopted by the PLT Group for the Palestinian liberation theology movement.

Once the name Sabeel was adopted, we had to register it officially with the Israeli authorities as a nonprofit organization. It was registered as "Sabeel Ecumenical Liberation Theology Center in Jerusalem." We were told that the official registration would take only a few weeks, but when several months elapsed, I sought the help of a lawyer friend who expedited the process and finalized the registration.

Once the official registration was completed, we started to prepare for our second international conference.

The Early Days of Sabeel

It was a very simple and humble beginning, but we felt the guidance of the Holy Spirit. Bishop Kafity gave us the use of an office space behind MacInnes Hall at St. George's Close. Later, we rented a bigger building not far from St. George's Cathedral in Sheikh Jarrah, and we moved to it on January 1, 1993. Providentially, the building was situated next to a bakery on a dead-end street. People could buy their daily bread from the bakery and receive their spiritual and theological bread at Sabeel.

Cedar accepted a part-time job to help start the programs that would translate our new way of theologizing into practical programs that would help the people. The Iraq war was raging at that time and there was a lot of debate about the "just war theory." Most of our people had not heard of this theory before and did not quite understand or accept it as a justification for waging a war against Iraq or any war for that matter. A meeting on the subject was very well attended and the discussion so lively that people asked for more such events.

After that, Marc Ellis was invited to give a public lecture with two Palestinian respondents. It was a huge success and people were very encouraged to hear a Jewish theologian who believed that Israel has done a disservice to itself and to Judaism by pursuing its unjust policy against the Palestinian people. These public lectures continued to be held through a program called "The Study Circle."

From its inception, Sabeel's ministry was truly ecumenical. This ecumenism expressed itself in all of our programs that transcended denominationalism, beginning with the makeup of the staff. Over the years, we had local staff that belonged to all the various Christian denominations in Jerusalem—Orthodox, Latin (Roman), Armenian, Anglican, Lutheran, Coptic, Syrian, and others.

But parallel with organizing the programs, I was careful to start with the Sabeel staff training. Through interactive weekly Bible study and discussion, our wonderful staff grew in knowledge, leadership, and faith. Every Thursday at noon we worshipped together and shared in Holy Communion followed by a common meal. For years, Maha volunteered at Sabeel by providing the meal. The local programs touched the whole Christian community in Jerusalem—men, women, and young people. We organized Bible study, lectures, trips, retreats, fast days, and prayer services. I was always thankful to St. Stephen's Dominican Church that allowed us the use of their large church for our occasional services of prayer for the city of Jerusalem and its people, as well as for lifting our prayers to God when called for by the political situation.

Speakers' Bureaus and Visiting Groups

As Sabeel and its ministry became more well-known locally and internationally, many groups and individuals from around the world came to visit. In response to our growing number of international visitors we started the Speaker's Bureau, which, over the years, trained some twenty-five young college graduates to speak to groups of pilgrims and tourists who wanted to meet Palestinians, especially Christians, and hear their story. In addition to the college students, our staff, some board members, and other men and women from Jerusalem, Ramallah, and Bethlehem were the first to be trained and become active with us in speaking to groups. Later, when it became difficult to come to Jerusalem due to Israeli army checkpoints, we had to conduct more than one speaker's bureau training focusing on our Jerusalem residents.

Over several weeks we gave courses in every subject that we thought was important, including public speaking, and encouraged participants to focus on one aspect of the conflict, such as human rights or settlements, house demolitions, and others, so that they would be better equipped to answer the pertinent questions from the groups.

Many of the travel agencies cooperated with us and assigned a slot of time in their itineraries for our purpose. The international groups that came to Sabeel had varied interests. Most came as regular tourists and pilgrims to visit the historical and holy sites, but while in the country they wanted to familiarize themselves with the Israel-Palestine conflict. Others were church groups who wanted to know more about the Christian community of the land as well as the political situation. We also had student and clergy groups that, in addition to the political situation, were interested in finding out more about Palestinian liberation theology.

I am grateful to all the speakers who have faithfully given, over the years, of their time to speak to groups the message of justice and liberation.

Expanding the Ministry

Soon after, in 1994, we started the Sabeel publication, *Cornerstone*. It was published four times a year and addressed various topics that ranged from Palestinian liberation theology to relevant biblical, theological, and political issues. *Cornerstone*, edited for over twenty years by Cedar Duaybis, started as a newsletter introducing Palestinian liberation theology to our friends around the world, and was our vehicle to educate and advocate for justice and peace in Palestine/Israel.

At Christmas time, Sabeel was a pioneer in holding an ecumenical Christmas dinner for the Christian community in Jerusalem to which the patriarchs, bishops, and clergy were invited.

Another important event was the first youth camp we held for middle school students. It was a lot of fun and a great opportunity for them to get together from different places in the West Bank at a time when the occupation kept people apart through checkpoints and barriers. The time together helped deepen their faith, while learning about the history of Christianity in their land, about their culture, and providing time for them to share their experiences.

While Cedar continued to serve in a volunteer capacity, Nora Carmi was added to our staff, working at Sabeel from 1993 to 2010, during which time new programs were introduced, including the women's program, the clergy program, and the interfaith program. Sawsan Bitar began as an administrative assistant on September 1, 1998, and helped organize the first clergy conference at the Church of Scotland Hostel in Tiberias in 1999. Two years later, as a result of the restructuring of our programs, Sawsan took charge of the clergy program while Nora had responsibility for the local community.

In all of our programs, we felt God's blessings on our ecumenical ministry.

Sabeel Branch, Nazareth

In 1993, the same year Sabeel Jerusalem was established, a Sabeel Nazareth branch was formed. The city of Nazareth has the largest concentration of the Arab Palestinian Israeli community in Israel, so it seemed logical and wise to have a Sabeel center that would serve Galilee where the Arab Israeli Muslims and Christians are numerous. Nazareth is also close to Haifa, the third largest city in Israel where a large community of Arab Israelis live.

Providentially, Violette Khoury accepted to be a part-time coordinator of Sabeel's ministry in Nazareth and Galilee. Violette, one of the first Arab women to become a pharmacist in Israel, was gifted in languages. In addition to Arabic, her mother tongue, she was fluent in English, Hebrew, French, and Italian. Violette, with the help of Lana Mazzawi and other part-time women staff, organized many varied programs of lectures, workshops, local trips, and Bible and book studies for women, men, and children in Nazareth and vicinity. Many times, both Jerusalem and Nazareth coordinated special programs together.

Sabeel Nazareth has also held many meetings with Jewish progressives in Galilee. They've discussed relevant topics and issues that deal with life and challenges that face Arabs and Jews in the state of Israel.

One of the most effective programs in Nazareth was a series of visits made to various historical and holy sites in both Israel and Palestine. Most of the time, they worshiped with local Christian churches and then spent the day visiting people and places in the area. Sabeel Nazareth always shared in our international conferences, especially those that took place in Nazareth and Galilee. Under the leadership of Violette, Sabeel Nazareth had an active and dedicated ecumenical committee whose church representation included all the city's Christian communities. Violette remains a highly respected person in the Nazareth community and beyond. She has been a very effective speaker sought after by many Sabeel groups that visit Nazareth to hear her story and learn from the wealth of her experience. In 2018, Violette retired, but she continues to serve Sabeel Nazareth in a voluntary capacity.[2]

Sabeel evolved into an international movement. With the work of so many, Palestinian Christians were finding their voice to raise hope for an eventual just outcome after decades of dispossession and occupation.

---

2. Due to the pandemic, we had to postpone our event to honor Violette. On June 17, 2022, Sabeel honored Violette at Nazareth in the presence of many friends and family.

13

The Election of a New Bishop and Another Round of Church Politics

IN 1995, IN THE midst of Sabeel's founding years, the Diocesan Council (Majma) was organizing a diocesan election for a new coadjutor bishop after Bishop Samir Kafity announced his plans to take an early retirement by the end of 1998. According to the church's constitution, Bishop Kafity could have stayed for another five years. Two candidates were nominated for election, the Rev. Riah Abu el-Assal and myself. Riah won the election and became the third bishop in Jerusalem.

Although it was painful and difficult to lose the election, in retrospect I started to view it as a sign that God's will was for me to pursue Sabeel's ministry for justice and peace. With the establishment of Friends of Sabeel (FOS) around the world, the opportunities began to open up for me to travel, carrying the message of Palestinian liberation theology (PLT) not only to our friends but to communities around the world that would have been impossible had I been elected bishop.

In the immediate aftermath of the election, both bishops, Kafity and Abu el-Assal, decided that I should leave the Jerusalem parish and assume the ministry of our church in Nablus. I tried to explain to them that it would be my privilege to serve the city of Nablus where my father was born and the church where he was married. But due to our daughter Nevart's schooling at the Anglican School in West Jerusalem and its English curriculum, it would be wrong to disrupt her education. I mentioned that I would gladly leave Jerusalem and serve our church in Ramallah because, although difficult, Nevart could continue her study at the Anglican School. In those days, there were no checkpoints between Jerusalem and Ramallah and a number of students were commuting every day back and forth. Furthermore, since they were transferring the minister of our church in Ramallah to take my place in Jerusalem, it would make sense that I would be assigned to the Ramallah church.

Soon it became clear to me that the real issue was to send me as far away from Jerusalem as possible. Sabeel was expanding, and God was blessing it. Bishop Kafity and the coadjutor Bishop Riah were aware of the impact that the ecumenical ministry of Sabeel was having, and I believe they wanted to curtail it. Deep down, I felt that their intentions were, to say the least, not pure.

Around this time, it so happened that Bishop Edmond Browning, the presiding bishop of the Episcopal Church in the States, was visiting, and he met with the coadjutor Bishop Riah and pleaded with him to accept a reasonable solution that would not disrupt the education of Nevart and the ministry of Sabeel, but Riah refused to bend. Later, a special meeting of the Majma was called in Amman to decide the future of my ministry. The two bishops insisted that I should move to Nablus. I argued that I was not against moving to Nablus; it was the timing that was problematic. I insisted that it was wrong for me to disrupt the education of our daughter who had just started high school at the Anglican School. By then, Stefan and Sari were already in college. Sadly, except for one or two people, no one dared to stand up for the truth. The arguments continued, and then Bishop Kafity said that if I didn't go to Nablus I would be fired from the church and I would lose my pension. Hearing this, I asked to be excused. I walked out of the session to an adjacent room. I wrote down my resignation, returned to the meeting and submitted my resignation to Bishop Kafity. I felt that everyone gave a sigh of relief, and the meeting ended.

I will never forget the courage of Muna Khoury. She was a member of the Jerusalem vestry and was its delegate. She argued the justice of my case, but they did not want to listen. My last service at St. George's Cathedral was Thanksgiving Sunday, the first Sunday of October 1997.

Maha started to look for an apartment to rent outside St. George's Close. It took us several months to find a suitable one, but eventually we found an apartment we liked in Shu'fat, the first suburb north of Jerusalem.

At the time of our move, our Sabeel office was in Sheik Jarrah. In the summer of 2005, the office moved to Shu'fat and our apartment was conveniently situated within walking distance from the office. We lived there for seventeen years. By then both Stefan and Sari had graduated from college in the States.

In order to give space to Assis Suheil Dawani as the new pastor of the Palestinian congregation at St. George's Cathedral, Maha, Nevart, and I worshipped for one year at St. Andrew's Church of Scotland across town in West Jerusalem. We were welcomed by the Rev. Clarence Musgrave, and after one year had passed, we returned to worship at St. George's. And I vigorously continued the work of Sabeel.

Sabeel and Hamas

The Sabeel movement started in the nonviolent footsteps of Jesus Christ, the liberator. Another movement that evolved during the same time was *Hamas*,[1] but their followers chose the armed struggle as the means to reach their goal. The general resistance during the intifada was spearheaded by the Unified Leadership of the Uprising, a coalition that also advocated for nonviolent means of resistance, such as strikes, refusal to pay taxes, and the development of economic self-sufficiency, such as organizing women's cooperatives, cultivating home gardens, and, in the West Bank, organizing mobile medical clinics and giving "illegal" classes when Israel shut down the schools.

The two movements, Sabeel and Hamas, started marching through history around the same time. Within a few weeks, Hamas expanded rapidly and grew to become a very formidable organization. Sabeel, on the other hand, continued to witness to the power of nonviolence and urged people to use all available nonviolent methods of resistance to bring about the end of the occupation. Although Sabeel chose the more demanding way of nonviolence, we believed that only nonviolence could maintain the humanity of our adversaries as well as our own.

After the establishment of Hamas, various new Islamic movements and organizations rose up that emphasized armed struggle as the means

1. Hamas, an acronym of Ḥarakat al-Muqāwamah al-Islāmiyyah, stands for "the movement of Islamic resistance," and is a militant Islamic Palestinian nationalist resistance movement in the West Bank and Gaza Strip that is dedicated to the establishment of an independent Islamic state in historical Palestine.

for the liberation of Palestine, and the use of violent military force that they believed was the only language Israel understood.

Both Sabeel and Hamas were aware that the illegal occupation would not end without resistance. We differed on the means and methods. Resisting evil, injustice, and oppression is a must for the Christian. But we felt that the armed struggle was not a Christian option for us. For Sabeel, the way of nonviolence is the way of Jesus Christ, and this is the way we will continue to follow.

14

International Experiences

South Africa, the First Apartheid

IN 1994, CEDAR DUAYBIS and I were invited by the Theology Exchange Program (TEP) to visit South Africa. We arrived the last part of August and returned in early September. Since this was just one hundred days after the end of apartheid, it was a very exciting time to be there. Our friends from TEP had a wonderful program planned for us, primarily in Cape Town, Johannesburg, and Pretoria. We visited Fr. Michael Lapsley in his Trauma Center. Fr. Lapsley is a white Anglican priest who opposed apartheid and supported the liberation struggle in South Africa. He lost both hands and the sight of one eye as a result of a terrorist act but continued his work for justice. In 1998 he established the Institute for Healing of Memories in Cape Town.

We were shown two of the larger townships, Soweto[1] and Crossroads, and also visited with the Muslim Judicial Council. On Friday, Cedar and I were invited to the Clairmont mosque where Rashid Omar was the imam. We attended the Friday prayers and then Imam Rashid asked me to address the worshipers. It was my first time speaking to a large number of Muslim worshippers, men and women, in a mosque. I spoke partly in Arabic but mostly in English. During the prayers, I felt I understood the chanting of

1. Soweto is the former home of Archbishop Desmond Tutu and Nelson Mandela, both of whom went on to be awarded the Nobel Peace Prize.

the Quranic Arabic more than some of the younger Muslims. I talked about Palestine and Alquds (Jerusalem). I related to them how our Palestinian people live under the illegal occupation of the government of Israel. There was also a period of Q&A where we further discussed the situation in Palestine. When we were through, a group of men and women stayed, and we had lunch inside the mosque. I was very impressed by Imam Rashid and I felt great affinity and respect for him. I was thankful to God for meeting him and I admired his love and devotion to God.

Years later, Imam Rashid went on to do graduate work in the United States and earn his PhD from Notre Dame University. I met him again at Notre Dame, where he often teaches. The last time I saw him was in 2018, when the Kroc Institute, headed by Asher Kaufman, launched my book *Palestinian Liberation Theology: The Bible, Justice, and the Palestine Israel Conflict.*

During our visit to South Africa, I also had the opportunity to meet the well-known theologian Charles Villa Vicencio, who had played a central role in South Africa's Truth and Reconciliation Commission with Archbishop Desmond Tutu. We hit it off well together and I expressed to him my love for hiking. Looking at Table Mountain in the distance, I felt the urge to climb it and felt as though it was inviting me to a challenge. That night Cedar and I had dinner with Charles and his wife, Eileen, and we agreed to hike Table Mountain the following morning. We did not make it to the very top but to the level below.

This was my first visit to South Africa. Since then, I've been privileged to visit a few more times. I appreciated the long struggle in which the people of South Africa were engaged against apartheid, and I, along with many Palestinians, admired their courage and persistence until they succeeded in achieving liberation. One important factor was the massive number of people who collectively marched against the evil of apartheid. In every nonviolent struggle for liberation, mass activity, including demonstrations, is essential to create change internally and have an impact on public opinion worldwide.

I learned many lessons from our South African friends, including their experience in the nonviolent struggle, their tenacity, the commitment of their leadership, and the prophetic witness of some of the church leaders, such as Archbishop Tutu and Beyers Naudé, against apartheid.

A Sojourn to Canada

In 1997, the Anglican Bishop of Ottawa, John Baycroft, went on a visit to Jerusalem and the Holy Land. His visit exposed him to the reality on the ground. He witnessed firsthand the injustice and the oppression of the Palestinians living under Israel's military occupation. On Christmas Day, he preached a sermon in his Ottawa cathedral about his visit. The Canadian Jewish Federation was very angry and demanded an apology and a retraction. The bishop had a choice, either to back down and apologize or to stand firm by what he said in his sermon. He chose to affirm and uphold his personal witness of the injustice perpetrated by the government of Israel. He got in touch with the Rev. Robert Assaly, chair of Friends of Sabeel Canada (CFOS), and asked him to organize a conference in Ottawa on the Palestine/Israel conflict.

Several months later the conference was held, and a good number of Canadians attended. A number of us were invited to speak, including the Bishop Baycroft, Rosemary Ruether, Marc Ellis, Don Wagner, and myself. We experienced some pushback from the federation, and we had to have police protection. We told our stories and witnessed to the reality of the brutal oppression of the occupation. Marc spoke about what it means to have a Jewish theology of liberation in the face of the injustice of the Israeli government. I spoke about my own story of being evicted by the Zionists, at gunpoint, from my hometown Beisan in 1948. I also introduced our Canadian friends to Palestinian liberation theology.

One incident still stands out in my memory. During a question-and-answer session, a participant stood up and started to attack us verbally, trying to discredit us. I was ready to jump up with an emotional counterattack, when Marc motioned to me to wait. The discussions continued and then Marc gave a very thoughtful, comprehensive, and sharp response. Marc was at his best with his clarity and articulate use of words.

Our conference in Canada was tantamount to the launching of the ministry of Friends of Sabeel in Canada. Up to that point, the Jewish Federation seemed to have had almost complete control of the churches, which were, generally speaking, silent on Israeli injustice. Most of them were sensitive to their relationship with the Canadian Jewish community and were very apprehensive to disrupt that. In fact, we were told that on occasion, some churches would consult the federation before issuing any statement on the situation in Israel/Palestine. Our conference in Ottawa contributed to a greater courage on the part of some of the churches. I have always been thankful to Bishop Baycroft for his unflinching commitment to the truth and his courage to sponsor our first conference in Canada. Today FOS Canada continues to be active through its different programs and projects in educating and advocating for a just peace for all the people of Israel/Palestine.

An Encounter in Chicago

At one of our regional conferences in Chicago, I was invited to preach at the Lutheran seminary midweek communion service and was encouraged to preach specifically on the gospel reading, Luke 16:1–13, the parable of the Dishonest Manager. The chapel was packed with both faculty and students. Although I found the parable challenging, I managed to connect it with my message for a just peace in Palestine.

At communion time, I was asked to serve one of the chalices. When I was about to serve the next person, instead of taking the chalice to drink the wine, he just looked me in the eye and said, "You are the unfaithful servant that has come to tell us all these lies about Israel." And he walked away without receiving communion. For a moment, his words startled and stunned me, but I continued giving communion. As usual, the service ended with a prayer, a hymn, and the blessing. Frankly, I lost my focus. I hadn't the faintest idea who this person could be. Afterward, my Lutheran professor friend who had invited me to preach explained to me that the person was actually a Lutheran pastor from the Chicago area, who was from a Jewish background.

Years later, I was back in Chicago for another Friends of Sabeel regional conference and was scheduled to speak in a large church. We had several hundred people in attendance. My professor friend alerted me that "Larry" was in attendance. I gave my presentation as usual, and I believe the audience gave me a standing ovation. Afterward, I was surprised when Larry came and greeted me. He reminded me of who he was and then added, "I have left the ministry. I am working for justice and now I am on your side working for peace, and I am on the board of Jewish Voice for Peace." We chatted briefly; I wished I had spent more time with him. I gave thanks to God for Larry's new ministry and commitment to justice and peace in Palestine.

Zimbabwe

On December 3–14, 1998, the World Council of Churches (WCC) General Assembly was held in Harare, Zimbabwe. Three of us from Sabeel—Cedar Duaybis, Hilary Rantisi, and myself—flew to Zimbabwe, taking with us the Sabeel photo exhibit, *Our Story, the Palestinians*. We were given space in one of the pavilions for the exhibit. This gave us the opportunity to introduce to hundreds of WCC participants the Palestinian narrative in pictures and to witness and advocate for justice and liberation for the Palestinian people. On the last day, a parade was held with every delegation carrying a banner from their country/organization. Hilary had worked hard to produce the lovely, embroidered banner from Sabeel featuring an olive tree and the words Justice, Peace, and Reconciliation around it.

At the end of the assembly, we joined a group of participants and flew to Victoria Falls. That was a day to remember. Walking along the long route opposite the falls in the drenching mist arising from the waterfalls, our voices completely drowned by the thundering sound of the water, was a thrilling experience never to be forgotten. The day ended with lunch on a boat in a lake along the Zambezi, with hippos and huge alligators a menacingly short distance away, and then an interesting visit to an alligator farm.

The Cost of Discipleship

Over the years I have been blessed to know and work with many men and women who have had the courage to speak the truth of their convictions regardless of difficult consequences. In August 1990, Marc Ellis and I were invited to the Ghost Ranch, a beautiful Presbyterian retreat center near Santa Fe, New Mexico, to hold a one-week course on the situation in the Middle East, and, more specifically, the conflict over Palestine.

Among those attending was Tom Are, a Presbyterian minister from the Atlanta, Georgia, area. In June 1991, as an aftermath of Ghost Ranch, Tom invited Marc and me to his church for a week of lectures, which attracted people from both the church and the community. The experience of meeting a Palestinian and a Jew speaking together and interacting as friends left its impact on the community. Unfortunately, it also came with a price that Tom had to pay. Some members of the session (the church's committee) were not in favor of the forum. The session felt that the Palestine/Israel conflict was too controversial, and they did not want their church to be involved with it. Eventually Tom had to resign from the church after having spent multiple years in good and fruitful ministry.

Tom and I became good friends, and sometime later he visited us and saw for himself the injustice and oppression of the Palestinians under the Israeli military occupation. He had the courage to be prophetic and to take a stand for what is right and just. I wished that more pastors, ministers, and priests would possess the same type of courage that Tom possessed.

An Unexpected Experience of Ecumenism

Although I had visited Athens many times, I had always hoped to be able to visit those places in Greece associated with the journey of the apostle Paul. In 2016, the opportunity came to make the trip with my brother Saleem and my niece Henriet. The three of us met in Athens, rented a car, and drove to the places the apostle Paul had visited and established churches: Athens, Corinth, Delfi, Meteora, Thessaloniki, Kaval, and Philippi. When we reached Philippi, we found a beautiful hotel overlooking the ruins of the old city. We found an appropriate place where we sat and read the letter to the Philippians as well as the references in the book of Acts. When reading the account in Acts 16:13, what caught my attention was the reference to a river, but we did not see any river around. After breakfast at the hotel, we went to look for the river, and to our great delight, found it outside the city, a beautiful river, its water flowing steadily and peacefully. Since it was Sunday, it seemed appropriate for us to spend time in reflection, meditation, and prayer before we resumed our journey.

From a distance, we noticed a group of people with a priest who seemed ready to start their worship. Henriet, who is fluent in French, approached the priest, introduced herself, and started conversing with him. She mentioned that "my uncle is an Anglican priest, and we are here visiting." The priest immediately welcomed us and invited us to join them in worship. He explained that he was a Roman Catholic priest from Italy with a group from his congregation, and was about to say Mass. He asked me to say a few words to his group and welcomed me to concelebrate communion with him.

I could not believe what I was hearing. The good Lord had led us to this open-minded priest, ecumenically conscientious, and theologically inclusive and welcoming. I was greatly thankful to God and to this wonderful brother. We concelebrated in both Italian and Arabic. It was one of the most meaningful services I have ever had, sharing communion with these brothers and sisters.

When I reflect on Tom Are and this Italian priest, I have come to see them as prototypes representing the best that we hoped to see in the ministers of the gospel of Christ. Tom models the prophetic that dares to stand for truth and justice, even when it is risky, unpopular, and costly. The Italian priest models the best in ecumenism that understands the unity of the Body of Christ and the fellowship and communion in the Holy Spirit. Both exhibited the inclusive nature of the gospel and the spirit of Christ that empowers us to serve one another in courage and love. Both embodied the vision and ministry of Sabeel.

15

Relations with Muslims

As mentioned in chapter 3, "My Life in Beisan," I was not aware of any discrimination or prejudice between Christians and Muslims in our hometown. The relations among the various segments of society were good and neighborly. I remember vividly that during Muslim feasts, I joined my Muslim friends in chanting the coming of the *'Eid* (feast) from the minaret of the mosque.

This same spirit of friendship stayed with me growing up in Nazareth. Among the members of our Christ Evangelical Boy Scouts were both Christians and Muslims. We studied together in the same schools and enjoyed our friendship with one another without any restrictions. Although we belonged to the same Nazareth community, we knew our limits. When it came to religious affiliation, we were Christians and they were Muslims. We respected our Muslim friends and vice-versa. What was important was honesty and integrity, not religious beliefs.

Many years later in Jerusalem, due to the emergence of Palestinian liberation theology and then the establishment of the Sabeel Center, my ministry expanded beyond the limits of my Christian denomination. Sabeel's emphasis was on ecumenism not denominationalism. This meant working with the various Christian denominations of the land. But beyond the Christian ecumenical work lay the significance of interreligious and interfaith relations. It seemed natural that I should begin by cultivating friendships with the Muslim community in Jerusalem.

This was not an easy venture since I was relatively new in Jerusalem, and I was not originally a Jerusalemite. I was more familiar with Galilee where I grew up.

I started by accepting PASSIA's invitations. Due to my academic background, I found great stimulation in attending its lectures. PASSIA is a Palestinian NGO that stands for "Palestinian Academic Society for the Study of International Affairs." It was founded in 1987 by Dr. Mahdi Abdul Hadi. At PASSIA, I met a number of Palestinian academics, both Muslim and Christian. I was privileged to take part in PASSIA's forums and occasionally I was invited to make a presentation, especially in the area of religion and politics. I remember I was asked to write a paper that was later published by PASSIA on "Mary, the Mother of Jesus in the Gospels and the Quran."

Dr. Mahdi became a good friend, and he lectured and participated more than once in Sabeel's international conferences and witness visits. My relationship with PASSIA helped me in broadening my contacts with the Jerusalem Muslim community, including Palestinian politicians and academics.

During Sabeel's first stage of feeling our way into the Muslim community, we organized a number of lectures where both men and women, Christians and Muslims, were invited at our Sheikh Jarrah center. The topics and lecturers dealt with our life together in the Jerusalem Palestinian community and the common challenges we faced.

At the same time, we started a similar program for young adults. It brought together a limited number of young people to meet each other and to discuss the needs and issues facing their age groups. Both of these programs educated us and helped us determine some of the priorities needed in our prospective interfaith work.

One of the important areas that emerged from our discussions had to do with the schools' curricula. We became aware that there were serious discrepancies within the educational system. On the West Bank, the curriculum was geared to Muslim students without considering the presence of Christians. In Israel, the curriculum was pro-Israel and discriminatory against Arabs, both Christian and Muslim. This prompted us to launch a series of studies by qualified teachers to dig deeper into these issues. For several months we continued these study lectures. It soon became clear that we had embarked on a huge project that went beyond Sabeel's mandate and ministry. In Israel, therefore, we were satisfied with raising the problems with some of the teachers and officials. In the West Bank, however, we touched on sensitive issues that raised serious problems regarding religion and democracy. We met with Dr. Ibrahim Abu Loghod, the director of the Palestinian Curriculum Center, and he cautioned us to be careful in addressing these issues. We felt that it was too sensitive to pursue them at the time. We recommended that they should be taken up again in the near future.

In 2012, this topic was picked up again by Muslim and Christian educators at a seminar that took place in Bethlehem. The recommendations were sent to both the Ministry of Education and to the heads of the churches, and eventually some positive changes were made to the curriculum.

In 2003, the Palestinian leadership were asked to produce a Palestinian constitution. We were not aware if Israel was asked as well. It is important to point out that Israel has never had a constitution and it is unlikely to have one. Be that as it may, it was the Palestinians who were asked to create one.

Dr. Nabil Sha`ath, a very respected minister in President Arafat's government, was put in charge of the process. As soon as the first serious draft was produced, I invited a few lawyers and legal experts, and we studied the draft very carefully. We then formed our response and went to meet with Dr. Sha`ath in his office in Ramallah. A number of the Sabeel Board went together, namely, Samia Khoury, Cedar Duaybis, Jonathan Kuttab, and others. We primarily addressed two issues. Since the draft constitution was, most likely, based on other Arab states' constitutions, we were not surprised to see written that Islam was to be the official religion of the state and that the principles of Islamic Shari'a Law would be the main source of legislation. We debated these crucial points together. We made it clear that, as Christians, we did not mind seeing in the constitution that Islam was the religion of the majority of the people of Palestine, but we rejected that Shari'a Law be the main source for legislation in order that the democratic character of the state be expressed clearly. What surprised us was when Minister Sha`ath said that there were secular Palestinian Muslims who were adamantly against including Islam as the religion of the state. In 2006, Fatah, the main Palestinian faction, lost the election to Hamas and so the work on the constitution was shelved.

The Objectives for Interfaith Relations with Muslims

From the beginnings of our interfaith work, it was clear to me that we had three basic objectives, namely, understanding, respect, and acceptance.

Understanding: Building greater understanding between Christians and Muslims is our first priority. Although there was a historical period long ago, after the emergence of Islam, where Christians and Muslims were friendly to each other, the vicissitudes of life, the political changes during the last fourteen hundred years, and the governance of religiously fanatic non-Arab Muslim leaders led to intolerance, fear, and alienation between the two communities. By and large, the Christians withdrew into their own introverted life and became more sensitive and cautious vis-à-vis their Muslim neighbors. Consequently, ignorance of the other increased and intensified. Such a state led to fabrication of myths and falsehoods that, with exaggeration, turned into fixed stereotypes of the other. It was essential for us at Sabeel to begin by dispelling ignorance and falsehoods between our two communities. It was important to build trust and to re-discover the genuine humanity of the other as neighbors and friends who, though belonging to another religion, were nevertheless fellow Palestinians who belonged to our common homeland, Palestine. Mutual relationships and understanding are, therefore, essential to dispel myths and shatter stereotypes.

Respect: Understanding can lead to respect of the other. In spite of the difference in religious beliefs, a Muslim can become a close and respected friend of another religion and vice-versa. Respect entails valuing the other as a free human being who is born in a different religion with a different set of beliefs, yet able to praise and adore the One God, *Allah*.[1]

Acceptance: Acceptance understands where others are coming from, it respects their faith and their religion (though it is different), and accepts them as they are. True interfaith can deepen the faith of every person engaged in it. So, we can accept each other, pray for one another, and commend each other to the love and mercy of God.

Sabeel Interfaith Work

In August 2009, the real opportunity to launch a more organized interfaith ministry with the Muslim community presented itself when the Rev. Ibrahim Nairuz, the pastor of the Anglican church in Nablus invited me to give a lecture on Christian Zionism in our Anglican church in Nablus/ Rafidia. To my utter surprise and joy, the hall was packed not only with Christians from the various denominations of the city, including my dear

1. Allah is the Arabic word for God. Muslims and Christians worship Allah.

friend Abuna Yousef Sa`adeh, the Melkite priest, but also with Muslim men and women, most notably Sheikh Zuhair Dib'ie and other sheikhs.

In my lecture, I spoke about the history, politics, and theology of Christian Zionism. I pointed out its Christian aberrations and its dangerous beliefs regarding the scenarios of the end times, and the role the Jewish people were expected to play. My presentation was received well by the audience and the discussion afterward was lively and stimulating. I was invited to Sheikh Zuhair's home, where I met his family and had a wonderful visit with them.

I shared with Sheikh Zuhair my hope to start a Sabeel interfaith program with the Muslim community and requested his help. He was receptive to the idea and expressed willingness to help. Assis Ibrahim was also ready and excited to work with us.

We organized a number of interfaith programs. In November 2009, we organized a conference in the Golden Park Hotel in Beit Sahour, Palestine, very close to Shepherds' Field. We brought together Christian clergy and Muslim sheikhs. Small mixed groups of priests and sheikhs would sit at round tables and discuss common concerns and challenges in their local societies. Intentionally, we placed those who lived in the same village together in order to get to know each other and build closer friendships that could help them resolve interreligious problems on the local village level. Most of the time, we would suggest a few questions around which the discussion would center. Those meetings began to create a different climate of understanding and respect. We also organized various local meetings in Nablus, Bethlehem, Beit Sahour, Birzeit, and other villages and towns.

The significance of Christian-Muslim relations can be well illustrated in what happened in the town of Kufur Yasif in Galilee. In 1999, we were planning our annual ecumenical clergy retreat in Galilee when we heard that a tragic incident had taken place in Kufur Yasif. A Christian man killed his Muslim neighbor. In the past, such an incident would have triggered revenge and the killing of a Christian from the family of the man who committed the crime. It would have turned into an interreligious tragedy, with clashes between Christians and Muslims that could have included the destruction of property and the injury of many people.

Such tragic stories have happened in the past. At times, the family of the perpetrator would have been forced to leave and abandon their homes in the village and move far away. The life of the whole village would have been disrupted.

None of this happened because of the friendship between the Orthodox priest and the Muslim sheikh in Kufur Yasif. Abuna Attallah Makhouli was aware that the killer was a mentally disturbed person. He immediately got in touch with the sheikh and together they were able to quiet the heightened emotions and wisely contain the situation.

Due to the enormity of the tragedy, I thought we would have to postpone our annual retreat and planned visit to Kufur Yasif. We called Abuna Attallah and he assured us that things were under control and welcomed us to continue as planned. Several days later, an ecumenical group of Christian clergy from the various churches held our retreat as scheduled in Galilee and then went to visit Abuna Attallah and his friend, the Sheikh. Both of them relayed to us the tragic story in detail. We then went into the church and gave thanks to God for the priest and the sheikh and the safety of all the people. We had lunch together and then we all went to the Muslim bereaved family and expressed our heartfelt condolences. Interfaith relations can create friendships that can overcome and resolve difficult problems. I have always appreciated Abuna Attallah's ministry and the climate of good neighborliness and cooperation that exists in this wonderful town.

In 2010, I went with Sawsan Bitar to meet Dr. Jeries Khoury, the director of Al-Liqa Center for Religious and Heritage Studies in the Holy Land in his office in Bethlehem. We discussed the possibility of a partnership between our two organizations, specifically in our interfaith programs with Muslims. I recognized that Al-Liqa had more experience than Sabeel in working with Muslim and Christian academics. Sabeel's focus had been to bring together Muslim sheikhs and Christian clergy to create greater understanding and respect, while Al-Liqa organized encounters among academics and an annual interfaith conference. I explained that if we could pool our resources together, we might be able to have a greater impact in building a stronger interfaith ministry. Dr. Khoury had a couple of members of his board with him at the time and we had a good discussion on the pros and cons of such a partnership, and we agreed on the spot to give it a try. Sawsan, the coordinator of Sabeel's clergy program, was ready to assume the responsibility of organizing this interfaith program with Dr. Khoury and his executive assistant. We also agreed that all program expenses would be shared on an equal basis between our two centers. Thus began a new phase of interfaith relations.

One of the most important encounters took place during the first week of November in 2010 at the Intercontinental Hotel, Jericho. After a two-day retreat of Sabeel's ecumenical Christian clergy, we designated a third day for an interfaith encounter between Muslims and Christians. Sheikh Zuhair Dib'ie brought with him approximately forty sheikhs from the Nablus area and Dr. Khoury brought another thirty sheikhs from the Bethlehem area. With the Christian clergy, we were together more than a hundred clergy and sheikhs.

Our meeting started with two keynote speakers, the grand mufti of Jerusalem, Muhammad Hussain, and the emeritus Latin patriarch of Jerusalem, Michel Sabbah. Both emphasized and commended the importance of interfaith relations and encouraged us to continue holding such gatherings.

After lunch and coffee and a short rest, we divided into small groups for discussion. At every table sat the sheikhs and priests. They introduced themselves, talked about their communities, and for an hour discussed the questions we prepared for them that were relevant to interfaith, picking up from what the mufti and patriarch had said. We ended the day with a few reflections and impressions given by other Muslims and Christians. We took a picture together and we returned home with many interreligious ideas to reflect on. Later, we organized similar events in the various regional areas, both north and south of the West Bank.

In those villages where the population was mixed religiously, it was wonderful to see the interaction and friendships between sheikhs and priests strengthened, and their friendships and mutual respect increase.

It is important to point out that there was a time in Palestine when most villages had Christians living next to their Muslim neighbors. Unfortunately, things have changed. With the exception of a few towns like Bethlehem, Beit Sahour, Beit Jala, Zababdeh, Burqin, Jifna, Birzeit, and a few others, most of the villages no longer have a Christian presence. Over the years, Christians left their villages and moved to the cities or immigrated abroad. The number of Christians became sparser until they finally disappeared. With their disappearance, an important dimension of living together and respect for the other was lost. Some sheiks were not even aware of the presence of Christians in Palestine. In those villages, most Muslims refer to Christians as *Nasara* which is a Quranic word, and do not associate it with the word "Christian" that we use.

An Invitation to Islam

One of the touching moments that I experienced took place when two sheikhs wanted to see me in private. They expressed their appreciation for Sabeel's programs and for me personally. Then they said that they were called to invite me to Islam and that I would make a fine Muslim. I thanked them and kindly told them that as they feel satisfied in being Muslims, I am very satisfied in being a Christian and a follower of Jesus Christ. I also added that there is one common thing that unites us, our love and praise of Allah, our merciful and great One God.

Iftars[2] in Jerusalem and Bethlehem

On December 11, 2000, during the month of Ramadan, Sabeel decided to hold an iftar in Jerusalem for a few of our Muslim friends. We invited about twenty Muslims and Christians, ten from each faith to an iftar at our Sheikh Jarrah office. To our knowledge, Sabeel was the first Christian organization after 1967 to invite Muslims to an iftar in Jerusalem. We did it for three consecutive years, but when we discovered that the idea was picked up by the Anglican Archbishop in Jerusalem, Suheil Dawani and other Christian churches and organizations, Sabeel stepped back to allow other churches to continue this tradition.

The iftar is not only about eating and drinking; it is a gesture of respect for our Muslim neighbors; it is an expression of honoring them; it is about sharing hospitality with friends. It is a celebration of our religious diversity that emphasizes our common Palestinian spirit and solidarity in good and bad days. Ramadan brings us together to strengthen the bonds of relationships and neighborliness in working together for the same cause of justice and freedom.

A number of years later, Dr. Mahdi Abdel Hadi of PASSIA reciprocated by inviting Sabeel and other Christians leaders, men and women, to an iftar in the Ambassador Hotel in Jerusalem.

After our partnership between Sabeel and Al-Liqa, we started holding a yearly joint iftar during Ramadan at the Bethlehem Hotel. Our first joint iftar was held on July 6, 2014, with over one hundred Muslims and Christians present. This included a number of sheikhs and priests and laypeople. At every iftar, both Dr. Khoury and I welcomed our Muslim brothers and

2. Breaking the fast in Ramadan.

sisters and expressed our heartfelt congratulations on the coming of the holy month of Ramadan, praying to Allah that we might celebrate Ramadan the following year when justice and liberation have been achieved for all the people of our homeland. We wished them an acceptable fast before Allah and a happy *'Eid* at the end of the month.

Publishing a Book on Nonviolence

At the joint program between Christian and Muslim clerics in the Golden Park Hotel in Beit Sahour, Sheikh Zuhair Dib'ie asked me to consider publishing a book on nonviolence. He argued that most people in the West have stereotyped Islam as a religion of violence and war. It was important, therefore, to challenge those misconceptions. We discussed his suggestion further with Dr. Khoury and agreed to start working on this project. Several months later, the book was published under the title *Nonviolent Resistance in Christianity and Islam.*[3] We requested the Emeritus Patriarch Michel Sabbah to write about nonviolence in Christianity and invited a number of Muslims to write articles on nonviolence in Islam. Sheikh Zuhair had a leading article with a number of other Muslims. We launched the book in 2014 in various Palestinian universities, including Bethlehem and Birzeit Universities and Annajah in Nablus. Before I left Jerusalem to move to the States, Sawsan and Dr. Khoury continued launching the book in other places. When Dr. Khoury suddenly passed away during his visit to the Vatican in 2016, the project stopped.

Al-Aqsa Mosque, Third Holiest Site of Islam

Over the years, I was able to build good relationships with Muslim leadership of the Waqf[4] that looked after the Haram[5] area. Occasionally, Sabeel would request to visit Al-Aqsa and the Dome of the Rock during our international conferences or witness visits. I was thankful that our requests were

3. In Arabic: *Al-muqawamah Assilmiyya Fil-Islam wal-massihiyya.*

4. Waqf is Arabic for an endowment or trust made by a Muslim or Christian for religious, educational, or charitable causes. There is an Islamic Waqf, a Christian Orthodox Waqf, Anglican, Latin, etc.

5. Al-Haram al-Sharif, the Noble Sanctuary, located in Jerusalem's Old City, encloses over thirty-five acres of fountains, gardens, buildings, and domes. At its southernmost end is Al-Aqsa Mosque and at its center the Dome of the Rock.

never refused. There was a trust relationship between us. They knew that as Palestinians we, Muslims and Christians, were working together against the illegal occupation of our homeland, Palestine. They always facilitated our visits into the Haram even when these holy places were closed to the general tourists. There was mutual respect between the Muslim leadership and Sabeel.

One of the difficulties we faced at Sabeel was our inability to find religious Muslim sheikhs who spoke English well. Many of our visiting groups wished to hear a Muslim speaker talking about his faith in English as well as explaining the political situation on the ground. The Muslim community had many academics who spoke good English, but most of them were not trained in religion and were hesitant to speak about Islam from a religious perspective.

The exception was Dr. Mustafa Abu Sway, who studied in the States and was himself a sheikh. He was always kind in accepting our invitations and speaking to Sabeel's groups as well as in our international conferences. Sheikh Mustafa is a person of integrity. He is a good representative of his Islamic faith and very knowledgeable about the political situation in our country as well as the racist system of oppression imposed by the Israeli government on the Palestinian people.

An Event in Denmark

In 2009, Jerusalem was voted by the Arab League as the Arab capital of culture. During that year a number of cultural events were celebrated in various parts of the world. As part of this celebration, a three-person delegation from Jerusalem was invited to visit Copenhagen, Denmark. I was privileged to accompany the grand mufti of Jerusalem, Sheikh Muhammad Husain, and Mr. Adnan Hussainy, the Palestinian governor of Jerusalem. We were received officially in Denmark and were invited to speak in various venues about East Jerusalem and its Palestinian people. We talked about interfaith relations between Christians and Muslims and the difficult challenges that confront the daily life of our people. We emphasized Israeli government policies in Jerusalem and the dangers of the Israeli Judaization of the city and the forced depletion of its Palestinian inhabitants. We had a number of opportunities to meet with the local Palestinian and Arab community in Denmark.

The Importance of Continuing Interfaith Ministry

Our interfaith work with our Muslim brothers and sisters has been fruitful to some extent but it is in need of greater diligence and continuity. There is so much to do, to cultivate, and to build, but neither Sabeel nor Al-Liqa has the staff, energy, or the resources to make interfaith a strong focus of our ministry. In spite of our modest achievements, the door to interfaith must remain open. The potential of a deeper and broader interfaith ministry is huge. It only needs the human and financial resources to build on the strong foundations that Sabeel and Al-Liqa have already laid.

There are wonderful people like Sheikh Zuhair and Sheikh Mustafa and many others who are open and willing to walk with us on the road of interfaith relations. This work is essential and of utmost importance in order to create greater understanding, respect, and acceptance between our two Palestinian communities, so that together we can give praise and adoration to the one merciful and loving God, our creator and sustainer.

Allahu Akbar

It is worth mentioning that the most often-repeated words of Muslims are *Allahu Akbar*. People often translate them as "God is great." A more precise translation is "God is greater." This is not a simple cliché; it is a profound cry from the heart of an oppressed people that Allah, God, not the people of power in Israel who oppress and scorn us, will ultimately triumph.

In such moments when our people are coerced and tormented, when we feel weak, hopeless, and helpless, all that we can say is *Allahu Akbar*. We are sending a strong message to our oppressors that they are not in control. God is in control, and our trust will remain strong in the power of God. Sovereignty belongs to God alone. God is the only sovereign and our liberator, and to God alone belongs all majesty and power forever.

16

Relations with Jews

DURING THE FIRST ELEVEN years of my life, because there was no resident Jewish community in Beisan, I had no experience with Jewish people. My first encounter with Jews was when I watched Jewish soldiers coming through Beisan to occupy it. I still remember when the soldier put his gun in my face to prevent me and my sister Naomi from returning to our home where my mother was waiting for us, the day we were forcefully expelled.

That was the beginning of my experience with Jewish people. They were soldiers and occupiers of our home and country. Later in Nazareth, it became a common sight to see Jews in positions of power and authority. I tried to avoid them as much as possible, but occasionally I had to queue in the police station in order to get a military permit to leave Nazareth, especially when I wanted to go to Haifa. Slowly it became the new norm to live under Jewish Israeli authority, but with the exception of official matters, I stayed away from them.

It is very important to distinguish between the ideological hard-core Zionists who viewed the Palestinians as thorns in their flesh and wished they would disappear, and those wonderful Jews of conscience who are willing to take a stand for the rights of the other.

There were a few exceptions at the time. One was Mrs. Gruber, the Holocaust survivor who came to Shefa Amer to teach piano to our children (see my story with Mrs. Gruber in chapter 7). She was different. She was rescued from the Nazis by Christians in Europe and promised herself that as she had received kindness and mercy from Christians, she would pay back other oppressed people with kindness and mercy. So, she came every week to Shefa Amer by bus to give piano lessons to the children.

About the same time, I met Joseph Abileah from Haifa. He had a music shop, and I remember going to his shop to buy a used piano so that Mrs. Gruber could use it for teaching. He was a wonderful and kind gentleman. He told me his story. As a child, he attended Christian school in Jaffa during the British Mandate. He spoke Arabic like the rest of the kids and lived in an Arab neighborhood. He was very angry when he saw the Zionists forcing the Palestinians out of their homes in Ramleh and Lydda. I found him very sympathetic to the just cause of the Palestinians.

It was only after 1972, when I was assigned the ministry of St. John's Church in Haifa, that I began living and working in a largely Jewish environment. Even then, my official church ministry demanded Arabic and not Hebrew.

In Haifa, it was easy to discover many conscientious, kind, and wonderful Jews. The Jewish people of Haifa seemed to me the most progressive and tolerant among the cities of Israel. But it was in Jerusalem, after leaving Haifa, where my relationship with Jewish people started to take on a new and more meaningful character, both negatively and positively. Jerusalem exposed me more deeply to the oppressive Israeli occupation of the Palestinian people, but it also gave me opportunity to meet and work with some amazing Jewish men and women of integrity and courage.

Friends and Respected Colleagues

Marc Ellis was one of the first American Jews I encountered when he came to visit Jerusalem in 1987, a few months before the first intifada. Earlier, I told my story with Marc. Suffice it to say at this point, that I was amazed to meet a Jewish person who was concerned about the predicament of the Palestinian people and their suffering and oppression at the hands of the Israeli government. I was impressed by his knowledge of the situation and his courage to speak publicly before a largely Jewish audience in Jerusalem, and not only to lecture about it, but to write about it in his book in which he critiques Zionism and the damage it has caused to Judaism.

Marc went on to write many books. One issue, in particular, needs mentioning. It has to do with what Marc called "The Ecumenical Deal." This was noticeable in Western Christian-Jewish dialogue. These interfaith meetings could focus on any topic except on the state of Israel and its oppression of the Palestinians. Western Christians were made to feel remorse for past crimes against the Jewish people, most notably during the Holocaust, and therefore it was fitting that they walk the way of penitent solidarity and support of the Jewish people and the state of Israel. In the words of Marc Ellis, what was required is "eternal repentance for Christian anti-Jewishness unencumbered by any substantive criticism of Israel."[1]

Since meeting Marc, I have met a good number of Jews in Israel and abroad who are people of conscience and courage who have authored books and become sought-after speakers locally and internationally.

One of those is Jeff Halper. I respect him very much because he has eyes and can see. He left the United States and immigrated to Israel because he subscribed to a Zionist ideology. However, the longer he stayed in the country and the longer he saw the racism and oppression of the Palestinians, the more he started to reject and turn against it. Meeting face to face with injustice can be a good test of a person's integrity. He confronted the army and the Israeli oppressive system and was able to analyze and expose Israel's apartheid system in his writings. Consequently, Jeff suffered but he remained faithful to his principle of nonviolent resistance.

In 2009, I was invited to visit Japan by the Anglican church there. My Japanese friends encouraged me to bring another person with me. I reached out to Jeff and he accepted. We spent two weeks lecturing in churches, universities, and various communities. Although Jeff is a secular Jew, his commitment to justice and peace brought us together. Every time we spoke, we helped our Japanese friends to understand the reality on the ground in Palestine/Israel. We introduced our audiences to the historical background. Jeff's presentations included a heavy dose of the Israeli system of oppression and the grim prognosis of the future prospects for peace. He was critical of the two-state solution and was leaning toward the one-state. Although I believed that the one-state solution was ideal, I always tried to argue about the two-states as the most pragmatic and realistic solution, since it is based on UN resolutions and international law.

In my presentations, I brought in the biblical and theological side of the conflict and talked about Palestinian liberation theology. I felt that, in many ways, we complemented one another, and I was thankful that we were able to be together to strengthen our friendship. From my perspective of faith, he is a contemporary prophetic voice that has been crying out

1. Ateek, *Justice*, 34.

against the oppression of the Palestinian people. For many years, he has been active in rebuilding Palestinian homes that were demolished by the Israeli army. In fact, the organization that Jeff started took its name from the rebuilding of homes: ICAHD "The Israeli Committee Against House Demolitions." The house of his close friend, Salim Shawamreh, was demolished seven times and rebuilt. Recognizing that they would never again be allowed to live in their home, the family dedicated it as a peace center—Beit Arabiya—to challenge the occupation.

There are many Jewish academics inside as well as outside Israel like Jeff Halper who have done the research and written books regarding the history and politics of the conflict. Ilan Pappe, one of Israel's New Historians, became well known for his book *The Ethnic Cleansing of Palestine*.[2] He documented the stories and experiences of Palestinians in the Nakba. Israel's Zionist narrative denied its crimes against the Palestinians and, instead, blamed the victims and negated their firsthand experiences. But Ilan Pappe found out that the narrative of the Palestinians was the truly historical narrative while the Zionist narrative was false and fabricated. Ilan has become a good friend. He has spoken a number of times in our conferences, both local and international.

Another respected Jewish voice, and a friend, has been Miko Peled who wrote *The General's Son*.[3] He has been a very effective speaker in exposing Zionist deceptions and correcting the records on the crimes and lies of the government of Israel. Miko is a person of integrity and possesses the courage to speak the truth with boldness and candor. He has been supportive of the BDS movement (Boycott, Divestment, and Sanctions), and is a strong proponent of the one-state solution with democracy and equal rights for all the people of the land.

A major contribution to opening people's eyes to some of the exclusive and extreme beliefs found in some parts of the Talmud and Halakha against "gentiles" has been made by Israel Shahak, who was a professor of chemistry at the Hebrew University. I met him in his office more than once with some friends, a few years before he died. I learned a lot about his way of thinking, especially his analysis and critique of the dark side of Jewish religion. Such a critique is not unique to Judaism; unfortunately, every one of our religions has its dark side and it is important to possess the humility and honesty to expose and confront those aberrations. Although his 1994

2. Pappe, *Ethnic Cleansing of Palestine*.
3. Peled, *General's Son*.

book, *Jewish History, Jewish Religion: The Weight of Three Thousand Years,*[4] was controversial, I found it very informative and stimulating.

I found Shahak to be a person of integrity and principle. He critiqued Israel's self-perceived racial superiority and racism, and many of the religious anomalies, indeed crimes, that he exposed, we saw practiced by extremist religious Jewish settlers against the Palestinians while the Israeli army watched them being committed with impunity. Shahak believed in equal human rights for all, the very thing that Israel has been regularly violating since its inception.

B'Tselem, an important human rights organization, was founded on February 3, 1989, two years after the first intifada, by Israeli progressive activists who believed that Israel's occupation of the Palestinian territories should stop. B'Tselem's work emphasizes that all humans are equal in dignity and so deserve the same fundamental rights. The name itself is an allusion to Gen 1:27, "And God created humankind in God's image, in the image of God did God create them." During the beginnings of Sabeel, we worked closely with B'Tselem. We shared their belief that the Israeli occupation needed to end, and a Palestinian state needed to be established alongside Israel. We enjoyed a good working relationship, and shared resources and groups.

Another important organization that was founded in 1988, after the first intifada, is Rabbis for Human Rights. These rabbis describe themselves as "the rabbinic voice of conscience in Israel giving voice to the Jewish tradition of human rights."[5] Although I believe that some of these rabbis have been sincere in standing up for the human rights of the Palestinians in the face of the Israeli government's unrelenting violations, a relatively few of them have actually been fully engaged. Be that as it may, I have appreciated the commitment of Rabbi Jeremy Milgrom and, later, Rabbi Arik Ascherman. The latter worked faithfully against Jewish settler violence, the confiscation of Palestinian land, and for the human rights of the Bedouins. On a number of occasions, Arik found himself in harm's way vis-à-vis the settlers and Israeli army. He has been a conscientious advocate for the human rights of the Palestinians.

The challenge before Rabbis for Human Rights and all other wonderful Israeli organizations that are working for human rights is the importance of a more united front so that they can be more effective in stopping the extremist religious settlers from committing egregious crimes with no accountability.

4. Shahak, *Jewish History.*
5. "Rabbis for Human Rights."

An Interesting Encounter with Rabbis in Detroit

I was always looking for opportunities to meet more rabbis and discover where they stood on justice for the Palestinians from their faith perspective. At one of our early regional conferences in Detroit, I received an invitation from three local rabbis, two reform and one conservative, who wished to meet with me privately. I welcomed the invitation and asked them to choose the venue. The four of us met in a small café and talked about the situation in Israel/Palestine. For over one and a half hours we discussed with candor the various aspects of the conflict.

With no exaggeration, we were in basic agreement on what needed to be done in order for a just peace to be established. I presented a strong case for the two-state solution where a Palestinian sovereign state can exist alongside the state of Israel, and that Jerusalem must be shared in accordance with UN resolutions and international law. I emphasized that such a just peace can open the way for reconciliation between the Palestinians and Israelis. I felt that we shared a basic agreement for the resolution of the conflict.

As our discussion progressed, I felt that my initial tense feelings had disappeared, the level of trust between us increased, and we were engaging each other with greater ease. Just before we parted, I asked them frankly, "Since it is quite clear that we are basically in agreement of what needs to be done, why don't you invite me to speak in your synagogues? I would love to discuss with them how we can work together for peace." Their answer baffled me. "If we invite you, we will lose our jobs."

I have meditated on their answer many times. On the one hand, I fully understand their concern to make a living as all of us do. They have families to care for. On the other hand, why are the synagogues closing their doors on mutual discussion about the conflict? Many mainline churches have welcomed Jewish speakers who stand for justice and peace. A case in point are the various churches that have invited Dr. Mark Braverman, not only to speak but even to preach to their congregations. He has been welcomed and much appreciated for his openness and inclusive message. In fact, I dare to say that he has been more welcomed in the Christian churches than he has been in Jewish synagogues.

I believe that the Jewish community in the States, especially Reform Judaism, was for many years anti-Zionist. They emphasized the universalist character of Judaism and ethical monotheism, stressing the message of truth, justice, and peace among all people. Why can't they be open to share in a civil and decent conversation about such a relevant issue? Who is closing the doors of the synagogues? Who pays the salaries of the rabbis and keeps them silent and unengaged? Are there written or unwritten policies that prevent local rabbis from expressing their perspectives and feelings on the Israeli/Palestinian conflict? Are the policies left in the hands of the top echelon of Jewish leaders while leaving the rabbis for the pastoral and spiritual needs of their congregations?

Although I have discussed this with a few friends, it remains a mystery to me. My experience with those three wonderful rabbis was amazing. I was certain that if more rabbis were free to engage us, we could together play a more active role in bringing our Christian and Jewish people closer to justice and peace.

A Visit to Sabeel

Mark Braverman came to visit Sabeel in 2006 with the delegation of International Peace Builders. Nora Carmi spoke to the group and introduced Sabeel and its ministry. She talked about Palestinian liberation theology and gave the group an overview about the life of the Palestinian community under the oppressive Israeli government occupation. As usual, Nora led a stimulating discussion with the group.

It was Mark's first visit to Sabeel and the beginning of a new journey for him. Mark is an American Jewish psychologist and a person of conscience and integrity. Since that first trip to Jerusalem, he has visited a number of times and has lectured at Sabeel and our international conferences, not only in Palestine/Israel but in the States and beyond. As already mentioned, Mark has been invited to speak and preach in a number of churches in North America.

Nora recalled that in 2009, Mark came on another visit to Jerusalem. He expressed his anger and disappointment at the way Israel was destroying the moral values of its youth and instilling in them an arrogant and blind hatred. Mark was visiting a Palestinian family in Sheikh Jarrah whose house had been occupied by settlers, and its inhabitants had been kicked out and were cloistered in a small tent close by. Mark was struck by the difference in attitude between the young yeshiva students and the calm response of the dignified oppressed Muslim women in the tent. This was in the season of Hanukkah, the Jewish festival of lights. It deeply pained Mark to see this, and he sadly remarked: "The light is in this tent!"

Mark's book, *Fatal Embrace: Christians, Jews, and the Search for Peace in the Holy Land*,[6] is an important work for all those who are concerned about Israel and its future and at the same time want to see justice done for the Palestinian people.

Kadima Reconstructionist Synagogue, Seattle

One of the few exceptions in my engagement with rabbis was my experience in 2009 with the Kadima Reconstructionist Synagogue in Seattle. It was a group of very progressive Jews who invited me to speak after their Sabbath service. They too, however, were under great pressure to cancel the invitation. The Rev. Richard Toll and I drove from Portland, Oregon, to Seattle one Saturday without being sure that the invitation stood. We arrived in Seattle and stopped the car in one of the streets not far from the Kadima synagogue and waited to hear from them. After almost one hour, the rabbi called and invited us to come. We attended the Sabbath prayers, and then I was asked to speak. It was a wonderful occasion. We had a great discussion and a long Q&A. They invited us for lunch, and we stayed, and our discussion went on for even a longer time. I was very pleased and encouraged and hoped that similar invitations would be forthcoming.

In 2017, eight years later, I was invited again. Kadima was meeting in another location. In my remarks, I mentioned that the situation for the Palestinians was getting much worse with the increasing activities of the extremist religious settlers whom the *New York Times*, in an article in September 2015, called terrorists and pointed out that they were all Americans.[7] I also quoted a statement by Ayelet Shaked, Israel Justice Minister, saying that she prefers Zionism to human rights. Gideon Levy, in his article in *Haaretz* on September 1, 2017, quoted Shaked as saying, "Zionism is not just, it contradicts justice, but we shall cleave to it and prefer it to justice, because it is our identity, our history, our national mission."[8] I asked our friends at Kadima, how do you deal with such truth? It was obvious that the Kadima members were not comfortable with such words, but I did not feel that they were going to do anything about it. Although I liked these friends and felt at ease talking and discussing with them, I did not believe they were progressive or radical enough to publicly condemn such attitudes.

6. Braverman, *Fatal Embrace*.

7. Hirschhorn, "Israeli Terrorists."

8. Levy, "Israel's Minister."

Jewish Voice for Peace (JVP)

JVP was founded in 1996 by a group of American left-wing activists whose focus was the Israeli-Palestinian conflict. The group is inspired by their Jewish tradition to work for peace, social justice, and human rights. They are anti-Zionist and work for the end of the occupation by Israel of the West Bank, including East Jerusalem and the Gaza Strip.

Soon after its inception, JVP started working closely with Friends of Sabeel North America (FOSNA), and a strong partnership developed between them. On more than one occasion, they've taken a clear and public stand to defend me from accusations of antisemitism that have been hurled at me.

JVP has emerged as the strongest and most credible voice from within the Jewish community that is very critical of the oppressive Israeli policies toward the Palestinians. It continues to gain strength in numbers. Among their founders are Noam Chomsky and Naomi Klein, very respected advocates for justice and liberation of the Palestine people.

Rabbi Brant Rosen

I have left Rabbi Brant Rosen to the end of this section because I have come to view him as representative of a Jewish rabbi who is willing to take a stand against all odds.

Rosen was the rabbi of the Reconstructionist Congregation in Evanston, Illinois, for sixteen years. Some of his members did not appreciate his clear solidarity with the people of Palestine. When visiting Jerusalem with a group from his synagogue, he surprised me by coming to visit us at Sabeel. This is how we met. When pressure mounted against him, he had the courage to resign his job and left the synagogue and went to work for the American Friends Service Committee (AFSC) for a few years. Then, with a few friends, he founded (so far as I know) the first non-Zionist Tzedek Synagogue in Chicago in 2015 and became its full-time rabbi. The core values of Tzedek include advocating for Palestinian rights and criticizing Israel's unjust behavior toward Palestinians. In their prayers, they memorialize the Gazans who have been killed by Israel's wars. Instead of celebrating Israel's Independence Day, they commemorate the Nakba Day.

On several occasions of Sabeel programs in Chicago, Brant and I have made presentations on different biblical texts that have been misinterpreted and acted upon by the Jewish religious Zionist settlers in Israel. Brant and I have become good friends. On March 26, 2018, a mutual friend, Don Wagner, one of Sabeel's active leaders, organized an encounter between Rabbi Rosen and me in Chicago. Rabbi Rosen came with members of his synagogue, and a good number of Christians were also present. I raised a few questions that had been on my mind since my meeting with the rabbis in Detroit. Why has it been that rabbis, by and large, are not open to discuss with us the Israel/Palestine conflict from the perspective of their faith? Why are the doors of synagogues closed to such discussions? Is there a policy against such meetings? Who is ultimately in charge? We had a lively discussion, and although I felt that Rabbi Rosen was sympathetic to my concerns, these questions persist. It seems important to me that, although Palestinians are looking for the resolution of the conflict on the basis of UN resolutions and international law, I believe that, inevitably, those of us who are people of faith have something important to say about matters of justice, peace, and security.

I respect Rabbi Rosen's courage and his commitment to a just peace. He has been active with JVP and was the cofounder of its rabbinical council. To some extent, he reminds me of the prophet Micaiah, who I read about in 1 Kgs 22. What I wrote about Micaiah in *Justice, and Only Justice*, applies in part to Rabbi Rosen's integrity.

> Those who view events with an eye for justice are disliked and often hated. It is not success and fame that attracts them, but morality. It is not the powerful arms of the state that impress them, but God's demand for justice. . . . Men and women who look for justice choose to be free. They choose to be critical even when isolated and silenced as a result. They rank justice above popularity.[9]

I have always believed that in order to resolve the Palestinian/Israeli conflict, we need Jews of conscience and integrity who have witnessed and experienced the injustice and the oppression of the Palestinians at the hands of the government of Israel, and are familiar with the background history and politics of Zionism, to join and work together for that end.

The individuals and groups that I have mentioned above are true representatives of Jews of conscience. They have been lifting a prophetic voice that has exposed the atrocities of Israel against the Palestinians. I am thankful for their courage, integrity, and commitment, and I only hope that by working together they can exert pressure on the government of Israel to

9. Ateek, *Justice*, 90.

respect and implement the demands of international law as the best prospect for a just peace so that all the people of Palestine-Israel can live as neighbors in peace and security.

17

Beware of the Slippery
Slope toward Racism

By the time the second intifada started in 2000, and through the following decade, Sabeel had become an international movement with several Friends of Sabeel chapters having been organized in the US, Canada, UK, Sweden, Norway, Denmark, the Netherlands, Germany, France, Ireland, and Australia/New Zealand. I have shared some of my travels that led to the beginnings of some of these chapters. Part of our success could be measured through the enthusiastic attendance at our international conferences held in Jerusalem, Bethlehem, and parts of the West Bank and Israel between 1990 and 2017.

One conference that stands out was in April 2004 with the theme being "Challenging Christian Zionism." There were more than six hundred participants attending from thirty-two countries. In the early days of Sabeel, I could never have imagined such an array of interest and enthusiasm. Notable speakers were assembled, including theologians, religious leaders, and peace activists who spoke of the heretical teachings of Christian Zionism. I was taken back to my college days in Texas when I first encountered some Christian believers who shared with me a theology which I later came to know as Christian Zionism. According to this theology, Palestinians were an inconvenience to the Jews' "rightful" claim to all the land. It also taught that when Armageddon strikes, two-thirds of the Jewish people would be destroyed and the last third would accept Jesus as the true messiah, i.e., would be converted to the Christian faith. How could reasonable people believe such a dangerous cultic theology? A statement released at the end of the conference stated that Christian Zionism "places an emphasis on apocalyptic events leading to the end of history rather than living Christ's love and justice. . . . We categorically reject Christian Zionist doctrines as a false teaching that undermines the biblical message of love, mercy and justice."[1]

One immense disappointment was the last-minute cancellation by the Archbishop of Canterbury, Rowan Williams, who had been scheduled to address the conference. In his place, he sent his ecumenical secretary to read a paper he had written. The paper did not even address any of the injustices of the Israeli occupation. Sadly, the voices of Christian leaders abroad and even in Jerusalem have so often been tepid down through the years until this present day. The great exception was Archbishop Desmond Tutu, the patron of Sabeel International, who, until his death in 2021, never wavered in addressing the injustices and calling out Israel and its enablers for its policies of oppression against the Palestinian people.

The conference also occurred at the time when President George W. Bush said it was "unrealistic" to expect Israel to abandon their illegal settlements. Bush added that Palestinian refugees who had been uprooted from the land in the fighting between the years 1947–49 could not expect to be granted the "right of return." The American president was himself violating UN resolutions and international law. Here in Jerusalem we were having this immense conference while the injustice and oppression continued unabated. Israel operated with impunity. This was not lost on the attendees or the speakers.

Jonathan Kuttab, a founder of Sabeel, and who later served as executive director of Friends of Sabeel North America, said "the situation just gets worse." He took on Rowan Williams's disappointing message, saying it laid out the theological imperatives for recognizing Jewish statehood without recognizing the rights of people already on the land. "There was no reference to the people who had been displaced. Where is the Good News for the Palestinian people?" he asked.[2]

He added that the conference "brings together so many depressing facts it leaves us helpless and hopeless," yet he found some encouragement

1. "Sabeel 5th International."
2. Kuttab, "Open Letter," 304–7.

in the example of South Africa, where the apartheid regime was doomed because it was built on injustice. "Injustice in this part of the world can't prevail forever," he said.[3]

I look back at those days when Sabeel's message of liberation was thriving, yet the outlook for an end to occupation dimmed year after year. Although President Barack Obama started his presidency on the right track, he didn't follow up on achieving a just peace and was unable to complete the job and implement UN resolutions regarding Palestine.

The Evolution of Jewish Extremism

Since the establishment of the state of Israel in 1948, its multiple-party system has evolved from mainly secular socialist parties with strong labor and leftist political ideologies to largely religious parties that have become today right-wing in their ideology and radicalism. It evolved from a largely secular labor party coalition that was dominant and unopposed to a very feeble party, lacking in political power and influence, which is barely able to muster enough votes to pass the electoral threshold in the 120-member Knesset (Parliament). It regressed from a central position that enabled them to form successive Israeli governments to marginalized parties on the left of the political spectrum with very little political clout.

First Stage: The founders of the state of Israel, mostly secular Zionists, used two magic words that brought Israel world support and sympathy and became the rationale for the justification of taking, usurping, 78 percent of the land of Palestine. The words are antisemitism and Holocaust.

Second Stage: The second stage started gradually after the 1967 war. In 1973, Menachem Begin and Ariel Sharon, in an alliance with several right-wing parties, established the Likud party. In the national election of 1977, Likud won, ending almost thirty years of the rule of the center-left parties. The shift was so dramatic politically that it was referred to as a revolution. This was the first time in Israeli political history that the right-wing succeeded. With the right-wing parties in power, the rationale also changed. Instead of antisemitism and the Holocaust, the rationale became God and the Bible that stood behind the establishment of the state of Israel. Gradually, secular Zionism began to wane, and religious Zionism started to ascend.

3. Kuttab, "Open Letter," 304–7.

Third Stage: In the third stage, the new generation of religious Zionists grew in strength. Their grip on governance grew stronger. They expanded the building of settlements that started under Labor; they dominated the political scene and increased their stronghold in the ranks of the Israeli army. Many of their leadership moved into the settlements and made it their homes. Moreover, their brand of religious understanding dominated Judaism.

Many of us started to refer to them as Jewish Israeli religious extremist settlers (JIRES). One of their obvious traits became their militant hatred of the Arabs (they don't use the word Palestinians), and their violent assault against the Palestinian people, especially the farmers. Here again, the religious rationale developed further. In addition to God and the Bible, the rationale now included the Halakha and some of the most harsh and exclusive religious teachings found within the Talmud that place the Jewish people above all other people.[4] They believe that the Jewish people are uniquely special to God and that all other people and religions are inferior. The writings of Maimonides and other medieval Jewish writers are often quoted and interpreted against the Arab-Palestinians. The result has been more feelings of hatred and bigotry against Arabs, both Muslims and Christians. Many of these extremists have been expressing their beliefs openly and publicly. Furthermore, they do not believe or respect human rights or international law. They only believe in divine rights that are found in their religious books. What makes them dangerous is the fact that they enjoy political power and that many of them today are ministers in the new right-wing government of Netanyahu (November 2022). Among their beliefs is a desire to rebuild the Temple on the site of Al Aqsa Mosque, the third most sacred site of Islam. They openly talk of, and practice, a policy of "transfer" of the Palestinians from their land, which is clearly ethnic cleansing, and they believe that the killing of Palestinians is condoned by God.[5]

A demand for ethnic cleansing is found in Num 33:50–53:

> The LORD spoke to Moses, saying; Speak to the Israelites, and say
> to them: When you cross over the Jordan into the land of Canaan,
> you shall drive out all the inhabitants of the land from before you,
> destroy all their figured stones, destroy all their cast images, and

---

4. Brownfeld, "It Is Time to Confront."

5. For more examples of exclusionary ethnocentrism in Jewish sacred literature, see Ateek, "Development of Religious Thought," 47–58.

demolish all their high places. You shall take possession of the land and settle in it, for I have given you the land to possess.

This is the reality today. Extremism is not just found in the actions of fanatical settlers who are stealing land from Christians and Muslims even in the heart of the Old City of Jerusalem, and ousting Palestinians from their homes in East Jerusalem, which is considered occupied territory, but also in the fact that these extremists are receiving support from the Israeli government. The previous Netanyahu government was fully supported by another former US President, Donald Trump, who outrageously suggested Israel could annex the West Bank.[6] It is obvious that the intent of today's Israeli government is to claim all the land of Palestine for Israeli Jews.

Fourth Stage: Are we approaching the Amalek stage of the conflict? In March 2023, a Palestinian killed two settler brothers in their car as they were driving through the Palestinian village of Huwara. Apparently, this had been in retaliation for the killing of eleven Palestinians in Nablus a few days before. (The Palestinian was later killed by the Israeli army.) After this incident, more than four hundred religious settlers attacked the village of Huwara, vandalized and burned the town, killing one Palestinian man and wounding several others. The damage was extensive. Bezalel Smotrich, the finance minister in the new government, called for the wiping out of the whole village of Huwara. Since then, another government minister has also called for burning down Huwara, and an attempt has been made on five other Palestinian villages. Are we on the threshold of a fourth stage, slipping further into a new Israeli form of apartheid and racism? Are Smotrich, Itamar Ben Gvir, minister of national security of Israel, and their extremist settler followers already into a well-planned scenario, not only for the ethnic cleansing of the Palestinian Arabs but also even their ethnic annihilation? It seems that nothing will stop them since they believe they are fulfilling "God's divine command" as recorded in Deut 7:1–3.

> [Moses said to the Israelites]: "When the LORD your God brings you into the land that you are about to enter and occupy . . . and when the LORD your God gives them [seven nations] over to you and you defeat them, then you must utterly destroy them. Make no covenant with them and show them no mercy."

---

6. For more information on religious extremism, see Ateek, *Challenging Religious Extremism.*

Have the Palestinian Arabs become today's hated Amalekites whose extermination "God" commanded?[7] We need to remember that the Amalekites have come to symbolize evil and represent the archetypical enemy of Jews. Such fanatical religiosity can be very dangerous and can threaten any future peace and well-being among neighbors, actually shutting the door on any reasonable basis for peace and stability.

If this is the case, then we are not alone in our struggle against these extremists. We must look to all Jews of conscience, whether Orthodox, conservative, or Reform to join us in this struggle, because this is their own fight and struggle as well. It is true that under pressure, Smotrich withdrew his demand to eradicate Huwara, but it remains the solution that he is thinking and planning for. The fourth stage is the age of the Amalek complex. The battle has gone beyond the political; it has become theological and spiritual. We appeal to Jews of conscience and to the international community to help us resolve this serious issue. This insanity must stop. The Palestinians are resilient. This is their homeland. These religious extremists have not learned the lessons of exile. If they want to live in peace with their neighbors, they have to shed their racist theology and learn to transform their hatred into love of neighbor. There is no other alternative. It is only the "meek who will inherit the land" (Ps 37:10–11).

7. 1 Sam 15:2–3, 7, 9, 22–23, 33.

18

"Seek Peace and Pursue It"

(Psalm 34:14; 1 Peter 3:10–12)

SINCE SOME MAY NOT have read my books on liberation theology, I offer some thoughts on that subject in the context of the present reality that hopefully will assist in understanding and, perhaps, creating a possible way forward for the two peoples to share the historic land of Palestine.

Understanding the Theology of Liberation (PLT)—The Tribal Triangle

After the publication of my book *Justice, and Only Justice*, I set out to expand and elaborate on PLT, not in the philosophical and systematic sense, but in the biblical and pastoral sense. My prayer was that the Holy Spirit would guide me to articulate a practical theology for the Christian community that could help it in maintaining and sustaining its faith in the midst of the perplexing biblical abuse by both the Jewish religious Zionist extremists who are fixed on the destruction of the Palestinian people, and the Christian Zionist extremists who are determined to expedite the second coming of Christ, even at the expense of the death of millions of people.

I am thankful that I ended up with a trilogy of books[1] in which I simply elaborated this PLT so that my Palestinian brothers and sisters, as well as others, would find this helpful for their life of faith. I also hope that

---

1. Ateek, *Justice*; Ateek, *Palestinian Christian Cry*; Ateek, *Palestinian Theology*.

future young Palestinian theologians will pick up where I have left off and continue to expand and elucidate other aspects of this theology.

How can I then explain Palestinian liberation theology? In ancient times, in our area of the world, our ancestors lived a simple tribal life that revolved around three essential components, namely, the god or gods they worshiped, the people of the tribe, and the land of the tribe. It was like a triangle. At the head of the triangle stood the god/gods, then the people of the tribe and their land. People believed that their god owned the land and had given it or entrusted it to the tribe to work it and live by it. Since antiquity, the life of the tribe, positively or negatively, depended on the interrelations and dynamics between these three components within the tribe and vis-à-vis other tribes.

In many ways, biblical theology centers around the three entities of the triangle—namely, God, people, and land. The history we study in the Bible is the story of the people who lived in that land, as well as the beliefs, the mores, and the ethical standards that existed between them and other tribes.

In expressing a Palestinian theology of liberation amid the Palestine/Israel conflict and the abuse of biblical interpretation, I was wrestling with the three basic entities or components of the triangle. In light of the Bible and my Christian faith, how do I understand the concepts of God, the people of God, and the land today? Most importantly, my basic understanding of God has come to me through Jesus Christ as the God of love, justice, mercy, and liberation.

This is what I have written about in my books. My intention has been simple and straightforward, namely, to help both friends and adversaries acquire an honest (as honest and truthful as I can be before God), political, religious, and theological account of the conflict over Palestine that might help them commit themselves to work for a just resolution. The objective is clear. We must achieve a just peace so that Israelis and Palestinians can live together in peace and security.

Let me briefly summarize these three components:

God: In the early books of the Bible, God is presented as a tribal god of the ancient Israelites. They accepted the reality of the presence of other gods for other tribes in Canaan and for other nations and empires in the Middle East. Every god had a name and belonged specifically to some tribe or land. The god of the Israelites' name was Yahweh. For them, God was so holy that they only referred to their God as the LORD. They believed that their God was the greatest among and above all gods. During the period of the exile in Babylon and Persia, people's understanding of God developed further, to the point that God was not only the greatest among the gods but was the only true and authentic God, the creator and maker of the world. All other gods were idols. This was expressed in multiple psalms. As an illustration, consider Ps 95:1–3 and 96:4–5:

Psalm 95:1–3 (NRSV)
1 O come, let us sing to the Lord;
let us make a joyful noise to the rock of our salvation!
2 Let us come into his presence with thanksgiving;
let us make a joyful noise to him with songs of praise!
3 For the Lord is a great God,
and a great King above all gods.

Psalm 96:4–5 (NRSV)
4 For great is the LORD, and greatly to be praised;
he is to be revered above all gods.
5 For all the gods of the peoples are idols,
but the LORD made the heavens.

Biblical scholars tell us that this recognition, understanding, and discovery was arrived at during the fifth century BC. When the book of Deuteronomy was finally completed, it was clear that people's response to God was to be expressed in total love of God. "You shall love the LORD your God with all your heart, and with all your soul, and with all your might" (Deut 6:5).

By the time of Jesus, the faith in the oneness of God was very well established and affirmed. From the gospels, we learn that Jesus contributed in making the love of neighbor as important as the love of God. He lifted up a minor exclusive injunction from the Hebrew tradition in Lev 19:18 and gave it a more inclusive and universal application. It became the second commandment of love, thus completing the two commandments of love of God and love of neighbor. I believe that these commandments constitute the heart of religious faith and action for all of God's children.[2] As Christian theology developed, we have come to know God's nature and character of love and compassion through Jesus Christ. And God in Christ helps us to see the world as an arena for the work of justice, peace, and liberation.

The People: It is clear in the Old Testament that the ancient Hebrews believed that their God, Yahweh, elected and chose them as his special

2. See how Jesus elaborated further on these commandments in Ateek, *Palestinian Theology*, 83–90.

people. Such a belief matches well the beliefs of tribal societies. This tribal concept also evolved and developed. Instead of being limited to a physical bloodline and to certain ancestry and tribes, it opened up to all those who believe regardless of ethnicity or race. Paul, addressing both Jews and Gentiles, said, "For in Christ Jesus you are all children of God through faith. . . . And if you belong to Christ, then you are Abraham's offspring, heirs according to the promise" (Gal 3:26, 29). The implication is that chosenness has to do with faith and not ancestry—that all those who believe in God are chosen.

The Land: The promise of the land to Abraham and his descendants was given in the context of a tribal society. In the book of Deuteronomy, chapter 2, God promised areas of land to the descendants of Esau and Lot as he promised the land of Canaan to the Israelites. In fact, God demanded that the Israelites respect the land allotment he gave to the Edomites, Moabites, and Ammonites, and not to fight them.[3] Such texts reflect tribal stories and legends. Concerning the promise of the land to the ancient Israelites, Walter Brueggemann wrote, "The land promise as we have it is in some large part the accomplishment of fifth-century traditionists, an accomplishment that became the bedrock conviction for the Judaism that followed."[4] In this regard, the words of the Church of Scotland Report are very apt. "To Christians in the 21st century, promises about the land of Israel shouldn't be intended to be taken literally, or as applying to a defined geographical territory; they are a way of speaking about how to live under God so that justice and peace reign, the weak and the poor are protected, the stranger is included, and all have a share in the community and a contribution to make to it. The 'Promised Land' in the Bible is not a place, so much as a metaphor of how things ought to be among the people of God. This 'Promised Land' can be found—or built—anywhere."[5]

---

3. Deut 2:2–9.

4. Brueggemann, *Chosen?*, 3.

5. Church of Scotland, "Inheritance of Abraham," as quoted in Ateek, *Palestinian Theology*, 103.

Three Pillars of PLT

First: The Inclusive Concept of Liberation

As Christians, we are used to saying that Jesus Christ is our savior and Lord. Such words reflect our faith in his saving death on the cross and his victorious resurrection from the dead. This is what we rightly believe. It is equally true to express the salvific work of Christ by using other categories of expressions. Jesus Christ is our liberator. He came to liberate us from the slavery of evil and death. As liberator, he can, through his power working in and through us, affect the liberation of others who have been subjected to the evil of injustice and oppression. This is true in the spiritual realm, but it can be true in the physical sense when the international community takes a united stand together through nonviolent resistance as I will later show. The apostle Paul puts it succinctly in his letter to the Christians in Galatia, "For freedom Christ has set us free. Stand firm, therefore, and do not submit again to a yoke of slavery" (Gal 5:1).

Today, the fundamental work of Palestinian liberation theology is the liberation of the oppressed Palestinians from the yoke of the Israeli government's oppressive system, and the liberation of the Israeli oppressors from their need to oppress their Palestinian neighbors. This means that both the Palestinians and the Israelis need to be liberated. This constitutes a priority in the work and ministry of Sabeel.

The concept of liberation theology must be understood comprehensively and should be applied holistically. It should encompass everything that enslaves and dehumanizes people, whether it is found in the political, religious, social, or economic spheres. It should include all segments of society. True liberation is a manifestation of love. Where there is love, there is liberation.

It is appropriate to apply liberation theology to the Palestinians living under Israel's illegal occupation, especially since the conflict over Palestine had, from its inception, not only political and economic aspects, but religious and biblical implications that contributed to the enslavement of our people by the Israeli government and continues today through its discrimination and racism.

The success of any liberation movement occurs with the active involvement of the whole community. I am thankful for the resilience of our people and their commitment to achieve a just peace no matter how long the nonviolent struggle might take. Many Palestinians are inspired by the examples of people like Mahatma Gandhi, Martin Luther King Jr., and Nelson Mandela. They consider them as models of commitment, courage, and sacrifice. Finally, our people live in hope that ultimately the liberation of Palestine will be realized.

Second: The Primacy of Nonviolence

For over fifty years, the government of Israel has been set to crush the nonviolent resistance of the Palestinians. Many times, Israel has instigated the violence that led the Palestinians to react through an armed struggle, and then blamed them for initiating the violence. I remember that in March 2018, the people of Gaza started resisting through nonviolence every Friday after the noon prayers. The Israeli army killed and injured thousands of men, women, and children, but the nonviolent resistance continued. Most Americans are not aware of the injustice and oppressive measures inflicted on the Palestinians by the Israeli army in Gaza, and by the Jewish religious settlers on the West Bank. By and large, the main American media does not cover the news of Israel/Palestine, whether by choice or due to complicity. Be that as it may, the Palestinians continued in their prayers to God and in their nonviolent resistance against the evil of occupation and the illegal siege of Gaza. Moreover, Israel continues in the demolishing of Palestinian homes under the pretense of the lack of building permits or due to proximity to the separation wall. In spite of all the unjust and immoral measures Israel uses to crush the Palestinian spirit and resistance, it has not succeeded. Our people's spirit and resilience are exemplary. Any policy to crush the spirit and morale of our people has so far failed.

From my Christian perspective, the way of Jesus is the way of nonviolence. Sabeel has advocated for nonviolent resistance in the footsteps of Jesus Christ its liberator. Resistance of evil and injustice is the right of all oppressed people. One of the most effective expressions of nonviolent resistance is through BDS (Boycott, Divestment, and Sanctions). Boycott was practiced during the civil rights struggle in the United States. It was also used by the anti-apartheid movement in South Africa. In 1994, Sabeel called for "Morally Responsible Investment—a Nonviolent Response to the Occupation." In 2005, Boycott, Divestment and Sanctions (BDS) was endorsed by Palestinian civil society organizations. It was also advocated by many Jewish Israelis (Boycott from Within), although in 2010 the government of Israel denounced this movement as a "national scandal." The BDS movement has grown among student groups, professional organizations, and peace and justice groups worldwide.

At the same time, it is clear that in order for nonviolence to have an impact, it demands the involvement of the whole community, including the international community. When people of conscience from around the world become increasingly engaged in practicing BDS, the campaign will succeed, even though it might take a long time.

Third: Justice with Mercy

The goal of liberation that we hope to reach does not entail the triumph of one side and the crushing of the other. The liberation we seek must affect the two sides of the conflict. Indeed, the Israeli injustice, oppression, and domination must end. The illegal occupation of all the Palestinian territories must be terminated. The Palestinian state must be established alongside the state of Israel. Jerusalem must be shared—East Jerusalem must become the capital of the state of Palestine and West Jerusalem the capital of the state of Israel. There must be a just solution to the tragedy of the Palestinian refugees based on UN resolutions and international law. Palestine must be free and sovereign as the state of Israel is free and sovereign.

Such a solution must be imposed by the international community through political means rather than military ones. In essence, this means achieving justice with mercy in accordance with international law. This can still happen if and when the UN Security Council members unanimously decide to implement its resolution 242/338, the two-state formula. It is possible that such a resolution might have to await the leadership of a strong American president who is willing to enforce the demands of international law so that a just peace can finally be achieved for the benefit of all the people of the Middle East. Such a resolution is not mere imagination. It is a real possibility, as Professor Richard Falk has shown in his two articles that he wrote in August 2019.[6]

Practically, Israel should start implementing UN resolutions by resettling all Israeli settlers living on the West Bank and East Jerusalem behind the 1967 Green Line in Israel proper. They would be replaced by the Palestinian refugees. East Jerusalem should become the capital of the Palestinian state. Other Palestinian refugees would be settled in accordance with UN resolutions and international law. I would personally add that legal

6. Falk, "Context Matters"; and Falk, "From Legitimacy Wars."

provisions could be made so that those settlers who wanted to live in Palestine, especially for religious reasons, and become loyal Palestinian citizens, could do so. Otherwise, they would have to move into Israel.

It might take a long time for such an implementation to take place, but there is no other alternative. Peace and security can be built only on justice as defined by international law. It is justice with mercy that can produce peace that can prevail, and peace can lead to security, and a secure peace can open eventually the possibility of reconciliation.

Although I have always believed that the ideal resolution of the conflict/dispute with Israel is the one-state solution, I continue to maintain that the two-state solution must precede it.[7] My assessment of the most recent shift in Israel's strategy is due to the growing influence of the religious Zionists within the government. They believe that the whole land of Israel belongs to Jews by divine promise and must not be shared with the Palestinians, who have no right to it.

It is true that the UN was unable to implement the two-state solution due to Israel's political influence on the US and its Western allies. Had the implementation taken place, it would have been much easier to deal with the negative results of the settlements. The UN and even some US presidents were aware of the dangers the settlement expansions would pose to the future Palestinian state. But Israel keeps pushing its illegal confiscation of Palestinian land and the construction of the settlements, regardless of the UN and international objections. Indeed, so long as the Americans do not force Israel to stop, it will continue with impunity. The Israeli government strategy has become very clear.

It is obvious that the key problem and obstacle for a just peace is the existence of the settlements. The religious settler extremists have won the internal struggle among the political Israeli parties. Is it possible to make Israel accountable for all its crimes against the Palestinians? I think the answer requires a two-state formula that precedes any eventual one-state model. Why?

I believe that both Palestine and Israel need time to heal. Both the Palestinians and the Israelis have experienced hurt caused by the other. The harm that has been done by both sides over the years has led to a worsening of the conflict, and as a result of these harmful actions, generations of Palestinians and Israelis have been negatively impacted. For over fifty years,

---

7. For more information on the one-state solution, read Kuttab, *Beyond the Two-State Solution*; and Halper, *Decolonizing Israel*.

Israel has tried to break the spirit of the Palestinians, and to some extent, it has managed to do that. Our people need to heal and breath the spirit of freedom. They need healing of spirit and soul. They need to restore their God-given humanity that Israel has denied them. They need to restore their God-given dignity, self-respect, and self-esteem. They also need to heal their psyche from the violence that damaged their very being and restore to themselves the spirit of kindness, compassion, and love of neighbor. These values need to be restored without the bullying and harassment of the Israeli occupation forces that would be all too present in a one-state formula.

Further, the occupation has also damaged many Israeli spirits and souls. Many Israelis need to heal their dehumanizing image of Palestinians. They must shed their feelings of superiority. Many need to recover their humanity. They need to learn how to live with Palestinians as equals, human beings created in the image of God and not, as in some of their religious literature, paint them closer to animals. They need to critique their religious exclusivity. They need to respect the equal human and political rights of their Palestinian neighbors.

Palestinian liberation theology will continue to inspire people and governments to practice justice with mercy. These goals are doable when adversaries are willing to live in peace and show respect for the rights and well-being of their neighbor. We don't seek revenge and the crushing of our adversaries. The Israelis will always be our neighbors. We want to live with them in peace, but they need to accept that in the twenty-first century, international law needs to be respected and implemented. For the sake of peace and security among people around the globe, the political and human rights of people and their neighbors must be respected.

Sources of Hope

Our patron, Desmond Tutu, said, "We are prisoners of hope."[8] The resilience of the Palestinian people remains strong. The declaration by three noted human rights organizations (B'Tselem, Human Rights Watch, and Amnesty International) that Israel has devolved into an apartheid state sets the stage for a confrontation with the continuing occupation. United Nations resolutions, human rights, humanitarian law, and the International Court of Justice remain on the side of the Palestinian right to their own state. Even Israel's greatest enabler, the United States, has shown fissures of

8. Giles and Jones, "Prisoner of Hope."

resistance in Congress, college campuses, and congregations in all mainline denominations.

Sabeel continues to make its witness of nonviolent resistance to the injustices of the occupation, not only in Jerusalem and Nazareth, but in all countries around the globe. These signs of hope are fuel for the witness ahead, however long it takes. Palestinian liberation theology is a compass that guides the movement of Sabeel today. As I write these final words for these recollections over the eighty-five years of my life, I am filled with appreciation for all those, too many to name, who have given and continue to give so much to this movement.

19

To God Be the Glory!

A Major Decision

In November 2013, during Sabeel's ninth international conference in Jericho, Palestine, we celebrated twenty-five years of the emergence of Palestinian liberation theology. In my final remarks, I stated, "It is time to pass the mantle to the younger generation. . . ." I felt privileged that with the help of a small group of friends and staff, I had been able to serve and nourish the Sabeel movement spiritually and theologically.

After a brief interval, and with the blessing of the Jerusalem Sabeel Board, I asked Omar Haramy to assume the directorship of Sabeel. At the time, Omar, a young Palestinian, had been employed at Sabeel for about ten years, and I had watched him grow spiritually and theologically. Academically, he had earned an MBA from the American University in Athens, Greece. Omar is blessed with a creative mind, a faith commitment, an ecumenical and interfaith spirit, and a willingness and ability to grasp the essence and spirit of Palestinian liberation theology (PLT). During our weekly Bible study, he always added fresh insights into the Scripture reading. With prayer and hope I felt guided to entrust him with the responsibility of the ministry of Sabeel.

While we were still in Jerusalem, Maha and I were already engaged in serious discussions about where we would like to spend our retirement years. Although both of us loved Jerusalem and were thankful to God for blessing our ministry at St. George's Cathedral as well as at the Sabeel Center, we realized that it was time, though difficult, to leave.

Since our three children were living abroad, it was natural for us to consider living close to one of them. McKinney, Texas, seemed a wise choice since our daughter and her family lived there. It was also close to where my sister and brother lived, as well as a good number of nephews and nieces. Maha also had a brother who lived in Texas. It was also a blessing that our sons, Stefan and Sari with their families, could come to visit us. It has been a great joy to be close to our children and grandchildren as well as to our extended family and friends.

Thoughts on a Personal Journey

Walking with God on the sabeel of life has had its ups and downs. Just because one is walking by faith does not mean that there are no hurdles or obstacles. On the contrary, it is normal and natural to live life each day and meet its challenges and opportunities. What has made it exciting and adventurous is the fact that I was not alone. This reminds me of one of my favorite stories in the gospels, the story of the two disciples on the road to Emmaus, not far from Jerusalem (Luke 24:13–35). As they were walking and discussing the current affairs, "Jesus himself came near and went with them" (Luke 24:15). So is our journey through life. There are times along the way of life when we feel Christ's presence with us, while at other times we don't. Nevertheless, he is always with us. I am reminded of an old evangelical song that I learned in the Nazareth Baptist High School: "He [Christ] walks with me and talks with me along life's narrow way." Or that lovely Christian poem where God walks with us, and the footprints are obviously clear. Then suddenly, there are only two footprints, and the person asks, "'Why, when I needed You the most, have You not been there for me?' The Lord replied, 'The years when you have seen only one set of footprints, my child, is when I carried you.'"[1]

Furthermore, looking back at my ministry, I am conscious of my weaknesses and failures, and the wrong decisions that I have made and the people I, undoubtedly, have hurt, and I ask for their forgiveness. In the words of the great confession in the Episcopal Book of Common Prayer, "I have left undone those things which I ought to have done and I have done

---

1. Stevenson, "Footprints in the Sand," 1936.

those things which I ought not to have done."[2] It was always due to the mercy and forgiveness of God that I was able to go on.

Walking with Christ is like having a GPS. There were times when out of sheer neglect, ignorance, distraction, or even rebellion, I have strayed, but Christ's GPS said, "Make a U-turn, go back; you are going the wrong way." I am thankful that I turned back. I am grateful that I was able to go back to the right course. And it is a wonderful feeling when, in retrospect, I was able to feel that I was back on the road with God. It is important to remember that in the journey of life there are times when God guides us toward new directions, new horizons, and new unchartered territory that we were not aware of or ever dreamed of going. It is important to follow the Christ GPS and that has been my experience, and it has led me to exciting adventures.

When I was ordained and became Assis, a pastor, of a small church in Galilee, I thought that I had reached my goal in life, only to discover that it was only the first station, the first bus stop, the first major intersection. The journey was just beginning. There were other important junctures that lay ahead. Some of them caught me by surprise, and now, in hindsight, I can see the hand of Christ leading me. In spite of the ups and downs, all that was expected of me was to keep walking faithfully, believing and praying that God would be glorified in the ministry I was undertaking. And I thank God for the presence of family and friends that were always there to help me.

After my father died, I was about to start my second year at the university. My mother found in his Bible a slip of paper on which he wrote, "To my son Naim, read Psalm 37:5, 'Commit your way to the Lord; trust in him, and he will act.'" This verse has stayed with me throughout my life.

It is only in retrospect that we can discover God's will for our life. It is only by retrospection that I was able to discern that it was God in Christ who called me from my youth to be Christ's servant. With humility, I can say that I am as certain as it is humanly possible that I was guided by Christ throughout my life's journey. But theologically speaking it was not I, but the grace of God that has led me. I believe that my call is captured by the words of a hymn I learned at seminary that became one of my favorites:

> I sought the Lord and after that I knew
> He moved my soul to seek him, seeking me.
> It was not I that found, O Savior true;
> No, I was found of thee.
> I find, I walk, I love, but oh, the whole

---

2. "Confession of Sin," 41.

Part IV: Sabeel

Of love is but my answer, Lord, to thee!
For thou wert long beforehand with my soul;
Always, always thou lovedst me.
—Anonymous, 1878

I testify that it has been the most wonderful adventure, and I am blessed to be able to share it with family and friends.

To God be the Glory!

Appendix

Sabeel International Conferences

- In 1990, a few years before Sabeel was formally established, we held our first international conference at Tantur Ecumenical Institute in Jerusalem. The objective was to introduce PLT internationally and locally. With the organizational and funding skills of Kathy Bergen, a Canadian Mennonite working in Jerusalem for the Mennonite Central Committee (MCC), we invited ten international theologians to the event, including, notably, Rosemary Ruether and Marc Ellis, and approximately forty local Palestinians. I introduced the concept of PLT to the local and international community and discussed my book, *Justice, and Only Justice*, which had been published the previous year. In the conference, multiple speakers responded to my book as well as to the importance and impact of the intifada.[1] With the help of Rosemary and Marc, a book was published by Orbis Books containing all the conference proceedings under the appropriate title, *Faith and the Intifada* (Orbis, 1992).

- In 1996, our second international conference was held at the East Jerusalem YMCA. The theme addressed the heart of the conflict, "The Significance of Jerusalem for Christians and Christians for

1. Here is a list of the Palestinian speakers that reflected a variety of responses: Hanan Ashrawi, Salim Tamari, Sameeh Ghnadreh, Jad Isaac, Don Wagner, Bassam Bannoura, Nadia Abboushi, Munir Fasheh, Geries Khoury, Elias Chacour, Riah Abu El-Assal, Jonathan Kuttab, Mitri Raheb, Zoughbi Zoughbi, Cedar Duaybis, Nora Kort, Jean Zaru, Suad Younan, Marc Ellis, Mary Schertz, Rosemary Radford Ruether, Mark Chmiel, Arthur Pressley, Mary Hunt, Ann Louise Gilligan, and Myrna Arceo.

Jerusalem." The papers were published under the title: *Jerusalem: What Makes for Peace!*

- In 1998, our third conference was held at Bethlehem University and our topic was "The Challenge of Jubilee: What Does God Require?" According to the year of Jubilee, all Palestinian land seized by Israel should be returned to its Palestinian original owners so that justice be restored. The book was published under the title: *Holy Land, Hollow Jubilee: God, Justice, and the Palestinians.*

- In 2001, our fourth conference was held at Notre Dame, Jerusalem. Since it was the beginning of a new century, we addressed the theme: "One New Humanity Where Justice Is at Home." No book was published.

- In 2004, our fifth conference was held at Notre Dame, Jerusalem, under the theme: "Challenging Christian Zionism." The book was published under the title: *Challenging Christian Zionism: Theology, Politics, and the Israel-Palestine Conflict.*

- In 2006, our sixth conference was held at Notre Dame, Jerusalem, and Nazareth under the theme: "The Forgotten Faithful: A Window into the Life and Witness of Christians in the Holy Land." The published book retained the title of the conference: *The Forgotten Faithful: A Window into the Life and Witness of Christians in the Holy Land.*

- In 2008, our seventh conference was held in the Golden Crown Hotel, Nazareth, and Notre Dame, Jerusalem. We addressed the Palestinian Nakba. We produced a number of shorter materials, including the book in Arabic and English where twenty Palestinian women and men shared their stories and personal experiences of their forced eviction from their homes in 1948. The title of the book was taken from a phrase by the Palestinian poet Mahmoud Darwish, *I Come from There . . . and I Remember.*

- In 2011, our eighth conference was held at the Bethlehem Hotel. The theme was: "Challenging Empire: God, Faithfulness, and Resistance." The published book retained the name of the theme.

- In 2013, our ninth conference was held at the Notre Dame, Jerusalem. The theme was "The Bible and the Palestine-Israel Conflict." The published book retained the name of the theme.

- In 2017, our tenth conference was held at the Bethlehem Hotel, the Golden Crown in Nazareth and the Boat Chapel at Magdala, the Sea of Galilee. We addressed the theme: "Jesus Christ Liberator Then and Now: Facing the Legacy of Injustice." No book was published but papers from the conference were published in issues 76 (Fall 2017) and 77 (Winter 2018) of Sabeel's publication, *Cornerstone*.

In July of 2013, Sabeel, under the leadership of Omar Haramy, held a Global Young Adult Festival in Bethlehem with the theme, "Moving Mountains, Re-shaping the World." Over 150 Christian and Muslim young adults from thirty-nine countries participated. The conference held a vision of uniting youth from different parts of the world to engage in discussion about human rights, environmental sustainability, economic justice, and community in order to reshape the world in a positive light by following the footsteps of Jesus. In addition to lectures and field trips, the group helped to dig a well at the Tent of Nations and also built two houses. The conference concluded with a flash mob performing the Palestinian dabke[2] on the steps of the Damascus Gate in Jerusalem.

---

2. Traditional dance of Palestine.

Photos

Photographed in Nablus, Palestine, 1923. Standing: Stifan
(Naim's father). Sitting: Nawart (Naim's mother); Naim's paternal
grandfather Salameh. Baby: Michel (Naim's oldest brother).

Sitting: Naim's father, Stifan. Standing: oldest brother, Michel. Baby Naim. (1937).

Dedication of the Church of the Good Shepherd—Beisan, Palestine, November 21, 1941. Pictured: Bishop George Francis Brown. The two small children in front are Naim Ateek (age 5) and sister Naomi (age 7).

Ateek family, approximately 1952. Top row, left to right: Huda, Hanneh, Fida, Naomi, Neda. Middle row, left to right: Naim, Hilda, Nawart, Stifan, Michel. Bottom row, left to right: Salma, Saleem.

1947. The last Diocesan Council Meeting (Majma') of the Episcopal church before the 1948 Nakba. Including Naim's father, Stifan Ateek, fifth from the left in the top row.

Old town Beisan market before the 1948 Nakba.

Naim at Hardin-Simmons University, 1961. Abilene, Texas.

Naim with the accordion (gifted by friend Doyle Combs in Texas) that
he used for his entire ministry and continues to play today.

Naim's ordination to the priesthood of the Anglican Church in Haifa,
1967. Naim with Archbishop Angus Campbell MacInnes.

Naim's wife and children. Jerusalem, 1986. Top row, left to right:
Nevart, Naim, Maha. Bottom row, left to right: Sari, Stefan.

Naim and siblings visiting sister Hanneh shortly before her death
in 1994. Top row, left to right: Saleem, Fida, Hilda, Huda, Naomi,
Naim. Bottom row, left to right: Neda, Hanneh, Salma.

Some of the Sabeel staff, board members, and close friends in the first
official office in Sheikh Jarrah, Jerusalem, in the late 1990s.

Sabeel-organized visit of clergy to Al-Aqsa Mosque with the mufti and Muslim leaders.

Sabeel-organized visit of clergy to the Druze community in the Golan Heights.

Visit with President Yasser Arafat in Ramallah, during a Sabeel international conference. Photographed: President Yasser Arafat, Hanan Ashrawi, Naim Ateek, and Presiding Bishop of the Episcopal Church Edmond Browning.

Communion during a Sabeel International Conference on the Mount of Beatitudes.

One of Sabeel's occasional prayer services at St.
Stevens Dominican Church in Jerusalem.

Members of one of Sabeel's international conferences.
Visit of Al-Aqsa Mosque, Jerusalem.

Archbishop Desmond Tutu in Boston at one of Sabeel's conferences in the United States.

Naim's wife and children in Celina, Texas, 2022. Left to right: Stefan, Naim, Maha, Nevart, Sari.

Naim's family in Celina, Texas, 2022. Back row, left to right: Sari, Naeem, Richard, Stefan, Lisa, Kristina. Front row, left to right: Tanory, Tristan, Nevart, Maha, Mariam, Naim, Markus.

Bibliography

"1922 Census of Palestine." Wikipedia. https://en.wikipedia.org/wiki/1922_census_of_
Palestine.

"1931 Census of Palestine." Wikipedia. https://en.wikipedia.org/wiki/1931_census_of_
Palestine.

Ateek, Naim. *Challenging Religious Extremism*. Jerusalem: Sabeel, 2022.

————. *Cry Out, Do Not Hold Back! Finding the Church's Prophetic Voice for Palestine-Israel*. Jerusalem: Sabeel, 2021.

————. "Development of Religious Thought in the Old Testament." In *A Palestinian Theology of Liberation*, 47–58. Maryknoll, NY: Orbis, 2017.

————. *Faith and the Intifada: Palestinian Christian Voices*. Maryknoll, NY: Orbis, 1992.

————, ed. *The Forgotten Faithful: A Window into the Life and Witness of Christians in the Holy Land*. Jerusalem: Emerezian, 2007.

————. *Jerusalem: What Makes for Peace*. London: Melisende, 1997.

————. *Justice, and Only Justice: A Palestinian Theology of Liberation*. Maryknoll, NY: Orbis, 1989.

————. *A Palestinian Christian Cry for Reconciliation*. Maryknoll, NY: Orbis, 2008.

————. *A Palestinian Theology of Liberation: The Bible, Justice, and the Palestine-Israel Conflict*. Maryknoll, NY: Orbis, 2017.

Ateek, Naim, Cedar Duaybis, and Maurine Tobin, eds. *Challenging Christian Zionism: Theology, Politics and the Israel-Palestine Conflict*. London: Melisende, 2005.

————, eds. *Challenging Empire: God, Faithfulness and Resistance*. Jerusalem:; Emerezian, 2012.

Ateek, Naim, Cedar Duaybis, and Tina Whitehead. *The Bible and the Palestine-Israeli Conflict*. Jerusalem: Sabeel, 2014.

Ateek, Naim, and Michael Prior, eds. *Holy Land, Hollow Jubilee: God, Justice and the Palestinians*. London: Melisende, 1999.

"Balfour Declaration." Wikipedia, n.d. https://en.wikipedia.org/wiki/Balfour_Declaration.

Barrett, George. "The Star of Bethlehem Looks Down on 750,000 Refugees in Holy Land; That Is Report of UN Children's Emergency Fund, Which Says Many Who Lost Homes in War Are Sleeping in Stables." *New York Times*, December 25, 1948. https://www.nytimes.com/1948/12/25/archives/the-star-of-bethlehem-looks-down-on-750000-refugees-in-holy-land.html.

Bibliography

Braverman, Mark. *Fatal Embrace: Christians, Jews, and the Search for Peace in the Holy Land*. Austin, TX: Synergy, 2010.

Brownfeld, Allan C. "It Is Time to Confront the Exclusionary Ethnocentrism in Jewish Sacred Literature." *Issues* (Winter 2000) 3–4, 7–9.

Brueggemann, Walter. *Chosen? Reading the Bible Amid the Israeli-Palestinian Conflict*. Louisville, KY: Westminster John Knox, 2015.

"Carter: All Israeli Settlements Should Be Removed." *Democracy Now*, August 28, 2009. https://www.democracynow.org/2009/8/28/headlines/carter_all_israeli_settlements_should_be_removed.

Carter, Jimmy. *Palestine: Peace Not Apartheid*. New York: Simon & Schuster, 2006.

Chacour, Elias. *Blood Brothers: The Dramatic Story of a Palestinian Christian Working for Peace in Israel*. New York: Chosen, 1984.

Church of Scotland. "The Inheritance of Abraham? A Report on the 'Promised Land.'" May 2013. https://www.scojec.org/news/2013/13v_cos/inheritance_of_abraham-original.pdf.

"Confession of Sin." In *The Book of Common Prayer*. New York: Church Hymnal Corporation, 1979.

"Demographic History of Palestine (Region)." Wikipedia. https://en.wikipedia.org/wiki/Demographic_history_of_Palestine_(region).

"Druze." Wikipedia. https://en.wikipedia.org/wiki/Druze.

Fairuz. "Bissan." Track 8 on *Jerusalem in My Heart*. Voix De L'Orient, 1967.

Falk, Richard. "Context Matters, Except for the Palestinians." *21st Century Global Dynamics* 12 (August 20, 2019). https://www.21global.ucsb.edu/global-e/august-2019/context-matters-except-palestinians.

———. "From Legitimacy Wars to the Politics of Possibility: Horizons of Hope." *Eurasia Review*, August 19, 2019. https://www.eurasiareview.com/19082019-from-legitimacy-wars-to-the-politics-of-impossibility-horizons-of-hope-oped/.

Farah, Assis Rafiq. *In Troubled Waters: A History of the Anglican Church in Jerusalem 1841–1998*. Dorset: Christians Aware, 2002.

"General Assembly Resolution 302 (IV)." United Nations Relief and Works Agency, December 8, 1949. https://www.unrwa.org/content/general-assembly-resolution-302.

Giles, Thomas, and Timothy Jones. "A Prisoner of Hope: An Interview with Desmond Tutu." *Christianity Today*, October 5, 1992. https://www.christianitytoday.com/ct/1992/october-5/prisoner-of-hope.html.

Gutierrez, Gustavo. *A Theology of Liberation: History, Politics, and Salvation*. Maryknoll, NY: Orbis, 1971.

Halper, Jeff. *Decolonizing Israel, Liberating Palestine: Zionism, Settler Colonialism, and the Case for One Democratic State*. Las Vegas: Pluto, 2021.

Hirschhorn, Sara Yael. "Israeli Terrorists, Born in the USA." *New York Times*, September 4, 2015. https://www.nytimes.com/2015/09/06/opinion/sunday/israeli-terrorists-born-in-the-usa.html.

Kuttab, Jonathan. *Beyond the Two-State Solution*. Washington, DC: Nonviolence International, 2021.

———. "An Open Letter to Archbishop Rowan Williams." In *Challenging Christian Zionism*, edited by Naim Ateek, Cedar Duaybis, and Maurine Tobin, 304–7. London: Melisende, 2005.

Bibliography

Levy, Gideon. "Israel's Minister of Truth." *Haaretz*, September 1, 2017. https://www.haaretz.com/opinion/2017-09-01/ty-article/israels-minister-of-truth/0000017f-dbbb-d3ff-a7ff-fbbbfadd0000.

May, Melanie. *Jerusalem Testament: Palestinian Christians Speak, 1988–2008*. Grand Rapids: Eerdmans, 2010.

Mote, Edward. "On Christ the Solid Rock I Stand." In *1064 Hymnals*, 1834. https://hymnary.org/text/my_hope_is_built_on_nothing_less.

"Muslims." Wikipedia. https://en.wikipedia.org/wiki/Muslims.

Pappe, Ilan. *The Ethnic Cleansing of Palestine*. Oxford: Oneworld, 2006.

Peled, Miko. *The General's Son: Journey of an Israeli in Palestine*. Washington, DC: Just World, 2016.

"Rabbis for Human Rights." Wikipedia. https://en.wikipedia.org/wiki/Rabbis_for_Human_Rights.

"Sabeel 5th International Conference Statement." Press Release, April 18, 2004. https://www.kairoscanada.org/wp-content/uploads/2012/02/Statement_Sabeel_ChristianZionism_18Apri04.pdf.

Sabeel Jerusalem. *I Come from There . . . and Remember*. Jerusalem: Emerezian, 2008.

Sayegh, Fayez, et al. *Time Bomb in the Middle East*. New York: Friendship, 1969.

Scholz, Susanne, and Santiago Slabodsky, eds. *The New Diaspora and the Global Prophetic: Engaging the Scholarship of Marc H. Ellis*. Lanham, MD: Rowman and Littlefield, 2021.

Shahak, Israel. *Jewish History, Jewish Religion: The Weight of Three Thousand Years*. London: Pluto, 1994.

"United Nations Partition Plan for Palestine." Wikipedia. https://en.wikipedia.org/wiki/United_Nations_Partition_Plan_for_Palestine.

"United Nations Special Committee on Palestine." Wikipedia. https://en.wikipedia.org/wiki/United_Nations_Special_Committee_on_Palestine.

Walton, O. F. *Saved at Sea: A Lighthouse Story*. N.p., 1887.

9 781666 798968